Bridge with a Feminine T

Bachelor Bridge, David Bird's
partnership with Simon Coche
reviewed by the leading British and American critics. This second collaboration, in the same vein, will be equally well received.

In *Bridge with a Feminine Touch* the intrepid heroine, Debbie, successfully climbs the bridge ladder. The adventure starts with her first game at the local club and ends with international trials and a glamorous match against the Polish ladies team. In between, she picks her way through a maze of exhilarating bridge encounters. An Italian boyfriend takes her to a midnight game at the *Piccolo Mondo*, a restaurant owned by his bridge-playing uncles. On another night Debbie and her partner, Nicola, surf the Internet, playing electronic bridge against unseen men from America and Sweden. The hilarity of the stories is matched by the superb quality of the bridge, which entertains and excites in the best Bird manner. What more could any girl want?

...dge fiction
... the Master Bridge Series

by David Bird and Simon Cochemé

BACHELOR BRIDGE
The Amorous Adventures of Jack O'Hearts

★ ★ ★

By David Bird and Terence Reese

MIRACLES OF CARD PLAY

UNHOLY TRICKS
More Miraculous Card Play

DOUBLED AND VENERABLE
Further Miracles of Card Play

CARDINAL SINS

DIVINE INTERVENTION

★ ★ ★

by David Bird and Ron Klinger

KOSHER BRIDGE

KOSHER BRIDGE 2

Bridge with a Feminine Touch

David Bird & Simon Cochemé

VICTOR GOLLANCZ
in association with
PETER CRAWLEY

First published in Great Britain 1996
in association with Peter Crawley
by Victor Gollancz
An imprint of the Cassell Group
Wellington House, 125 Strand, London WC2R 0BB

A catalogue record for this book
is available from the British Library

ISBN 0 575 06361 0

Photoset in Great Britain by
Rowland Phototypesetting Ltd, Bury St Edmunds, Suffolk
Printed in Great Britain by St Edmundsbury Press Ltd,
Bury St Edmunds, Suffolk

Contents

1 The Chelsea Pensioners

A few days after I had moved into my new London flat a free local paper dropped through the letter-box. Well, it would serve to line the cat's litter tray, I thought. My eyes strayed to an advertisement in the entertainment section:

> *Bridge in the community. Chelsea Town Hall, Thursday evenings at 7 pm. Friendly rubber game, all standards.*

I hadn't played bridge for two years, not since university. Perhaps it would do me good to get out and meet a few people.

The following Thursday I found myself in a large, shabby meeting room with high ceilings and ornate Victorian plasterwork. Six or seven tables were in play but no-one under pensionable age was in sight.

'Are you here for the bridge?' enquired a lady who looked old enough to remember the last time the room had been decorated.

'I'll look after her,' said a voice behind me. I turned to see a portly old man with a few strands of hair draped across his scalp. He seized me by the elbow and dragged me to a nearby table that was occupied by two other ancient men.

'I'm Arthur,' he said. 'This is Colonel Wilkes and that's Lionel.'

He released his grip on me and the circulation slowly returned to my arm. Arthur had definitely been a lawyer, I decided, as I cut to partner him in the first rubber. I could just imagine him in some Dickensian office, surrounded by pink-ribboned files.

Arthur dealt the first hand and opened two hearts. The Colonel overcalled two spades and I found myself looking at:

♠ 10 7 4 ♡ K 8 7 3 ◇ A 8 3 ♣ K 10 2

Was my partner's two-heart opening weak or strong, I wondered. Everyone over sixty played strong twos, surely, but perhaps if I responded three hearts that would cater for both possibilities. If he did have a strong two he would continue bidding and I could then head for a slam. 'Three hearts,' I said.

Lionel, on my left, bid three spades. My partner, Arthur, rebid four clubs and the Colonel went to four spades. These old guys certainly liked to bid! I had a clear picture of my partner's hand by now – he had a strong two in hearts, suitable for a slam, and the ace of clubs. Thanks to the opponents' bidding, I could also place him with at most one spade. A small slam was a certainty. 'Six hearts,' I said.

Somewhat to my surprise, my left-hand opponent doubled. It turned out that this was the full deal:

Love all
Dealer South

	North	
	♠ 10 7 4 ♡ K 8 7 3 ♢ A 8 3 ♣ K 10 2	
West ♠ A K J 8 3 2 ♡ 10 5 ♢ K J 2 ♣ Q 8	N / W E / S	**East** ♠ Q 9 6 5 ♡ Q 2 ♢ Q 10 6 5 ♣ A 9 6
	♠ – ♡ A J 9 6 4 ♢ 9 7 4 ♣ J 7 5 4 3	
	South	

West	*North*	*East*	*South*
Colonel Wilkes	Debbie	Lionel	Arthur
–	–	–	2♡
2♠	3♡	3♠	4♣
4♠	6♡	Dble	All Pass

Arthur ruffed the spade king lead and drew trumps in two rounds. A club to the 10 drew East's ace and the diamond switch was won in dummy. When West's queen of clubs fell under the king, the contract was home. Dummy's two diamond losers could be thrown on declarer's long clubs.

'Lead a diamond, partner!' exclaimed Lionel, who was wearing a thick overcoat despite the warmth of the room. 'They heard us bid spades and *still* bid the slam. It's obvious they were prepared for a spade lead.'

I looked in amazement at my partner. 'You only had a weak two,' I said.

Arthur gazed back triumphantly. 'Yes, we hadn't discussed it, but I know you under-30s like to play weak twos,' he said. 'I thought if I showed my second suit as well, you'd be able to judge how high to go.'

A few hands later Arthur had a chance to win a 700 rubber. Not that I'd be able to retire in comfort with the stakes at just 10p a 100.

North–South game
Dealer East

North:
♠ 7 6 3
♡ A
◇ A 3 2
♣ K Q 7 6 5 3

West:
♠ Q 9
♡ J 10 6 5 2
◇ J 10 8 6
♣ 10 8

East:
♠ K 10 8 4
♡ 8 7 4 3
◇ Q 5
♣ A J 2

South:
♠ A J 5 2
♡ K Q 9
◇ K 9 7 4
♣ 9 4

West	*North*	*East*	*South*
Colonel Wilkes	Debbie	Lionel	Arthur
–	–	Pass	1NT
Pass	3NT	All Pass	

I raised Arthur's 12–14 1NT to game (yes, they play weak throughout) and West led ♡5, won by the bare ace. When Arthur played the king of clubs from dummy at trick two the overcoated East won with the ace and played back another heart. Contrary to his expectations, no doubt, the defence of the hand was now at an end. Declarer won the second heart and continued with queen and another club. The diamond ace was an entry to the clubs, so he could claim ten tricks.

Colonel Wilkes tossed his remaining cards on the table. 'Damn-fool defence, partner!' he exclaimed. 'Duck the first club, like a man, and you kill the suit.'

'How was I meant to know your hearts were only jack-high?' replied an indignant Lionel. 'I thought we'd get it off easily.'

'So we would have done,' declared the Colonel, 'if you hadn't defended like a complete buffoon.'

We had won a 12-point rubber. Arthur and I cut out and the table was made up by two elderly women, one with a walking stick.

'Not the most tactful of men, the Colonel,' said Arthur, as we waited to cut in elsewhere. 'Typical military man – intolerant of the slightest error.'

I looked round to see where the exit was. One more rubber and I would be off. I had more chance of winning the national lottery than meeting an attractive young male in this setting.

'I don't mind people pointing out *my* mistakes, it's the only way to learn,' continued Arthur. 'But it should be done quietly, away from the table.'

'In that case, I think you might have tried something different on that last hand,' I replied. 'If you play a low club from dummy at trick 2, you can win the return and play a club to the king. You just need clubs 3–2 to make it.'

'I do believe you're right, my dear!' Arthur replied. 'My game's become quite rusty playing with these old fogeys.' He adjusted the strands of hair across his head. 'I'm nowhere near as old as them, as you can see.'

He produced a small pocket book. 'Now, you must give me your phone number and come round one evening for a sherry and a bit of bidding practice.' His eyes shone as he surveyed the decrepit room before him. 'You and I should be able to clean up in a place like this.'

I looked down at my watch. 'Good gracious, is it ten to eight already?' I exclaimed. 'I'll have to go, I'm afraid.'

Arthur looked so distraught, I almost felt sorry for him.

'See you next Thursday, perhaps,' I said.

2 *Homo Typicalis*

I knew he would end up at my table the moment he entered the room. Most men make a bee-line for an isolated female bridge-player; some with the eternal optimism of the predatory male, others because they think they'll get a good result or two. This particular specimen of manhood seemed to fall into both categories.

He was in his early thirties, with brown hair in need of a cut, and he was holding a full pint of beer. The way his bulging stomach competed with the restraining buttons on his shirt suggested that this pint would be the first of many. He swerved expertly past a number of tables, giving them token cursory glances, and finally came to rest at mine.

'Haven't seen you here before,' he said as he sat down.

'That's probably because I haven't been here before,' I replied sweetly.

'First time here, then?' he continued, with the logic of a player who draws an unnecessary extra round of trumps.

Nicola arrived, her customary one minute before the Ruffles Club duplicate was due to start. 'Craig's one of the club regulars, Debbie,' she informed me, giving him an unfavourable look. 'He doesn't regard any female as a full member of the club until he's played with her.'

'I don't get many dissatisfied customers,' declared Craig. 'There's nothing like playing with a good partner to improve your game.'

Craig's partner, a shy creature called Ian, completed the table. The pleasantries, such as they were, ended and the hostilities began.

Love all
Dealer South

North: ♠ K 9 5 4 ♡ 10 5 2 ♢ A J 10 3 2 ♣ Q

West: ♠ 3 ♡ K Q 9 7 6 3 ♢ 6 5 ♣ K 8 7 6

East: ♠ 8 ♡ J 8 4 ♢ K Q 8 ♣ A J 9 5 4 3

South: ♠ A Q J 10 7 6 2 ♡ A ♢ 9 7 4 ♣ 10 2

West	*North*	*East*	*South*
Craig	Nicola	Ian	Debbie
–	–	–	1♠
3♡	4♠	5♡	5♠
All Pass			

I started on the wrong foot by opening just one spade on my hand, eventually being pushed to the five level. Lesson learnt. Next time, I'd remember to open four spades, which would doubtless have shut them out.

I won the king of hearts lead with the ace and saw that the contract would be easy unless both diamonds were offside. If that were the case, I would need to eliminate clubs and hearts before taking the first diamond finesse.

It wouldn't suit me for West to gain the lead, since he might play a diamond through. To increase the chances of East winning the first club, it seemed best to lead the suit from dummy. I crossed to the spade king, both defenders following, then called for the queen of clubs.

All was well. The bespectacled Ian, sitting East, won with the ace and returned a heart. It was plain sailing now. I completed the elimination and finessed the jack of diamonds, end-playing East.

Craig, who had doubtless expected two tops from the round, glared at his partner. 'You *must* let the first round of clubs run to me, Ian,' he exclaimed. 'I put a diamond through, to your queen, and you still have a safe club exit.'

'I can't defend that way at pairs,' retorted his partner. 'She's opened the bidding; you've only made a weak jump overcall. Why should I place you with the king of clubs?'

'Didn't think much of your five-heart bid either,' persisted Craig. 'Why not five clubs? It must be fit-showing at that level.'

'What on earth difference would that make?' said Ian.

'If I know you've got club values, I lead the king of clubs,' declared Craig. 'Diamond switch stands out a mile once the dummy goes down.'

It seemed to me that he was talking total nonsense. Still, best not to get involved. On the next board Ian passed on my right and, at favourable vulnerability, I found myself looking at this less than glittering collection:

♠Q ♡85 ◇9743 ♣QJ10842

Yes, I know that pre-empts are meant to be disciplined in the second seat – I do read *some* bridge books. Still, I was determined to capitalise on our good result on the first board. 'Three clubs,' I said.

Craig drained the last two drops from his beer glass and overcalled 3NT.

'Four diamonds,' said Nicola. Could have been worse, I thought; she might have introduced one of the majors.

'Double,' said Ian.

I passed, quite happily, and Craig passed. Now Nicola redoubled – not such good news. If she thought we could make ten tricks in diamonds, she'd have been delighted to pass out the double. This must be an SOS redouble, based on some two-suiter in the majors. A less wild bidder might, just possibly, have been deterred by my three-club bid. Not our Nicola, though. I bid a distinctly unhappy four hearts and was not in the least surprised to hear a double on my left.

There was no more bidding and this turned out to be the full hand:

East–West Game Dealer East	♠ K 9 8 5 4 3 2 ♡ A 9 7 6 4 2 ♢ – ♣ –	
♠ A 6 ♡ K J 3 ♢ A K J 8 6 ♣ A K 7	N W E S	♠ J 10 7 ♡ Q 10 ♢ Q 10 5 2 ♣ 9 6 5 3
	♠ Q ♡ 8 5 ♢ 9 7 4 3 ♣ Q J 10 8 4 2	

West	*North*	*East*	*South*
Craig	Nicola	Ian	Debbie
–	—	Pass	3♣
3NT	4♢	Dble	Pass
Pass	Redble	Pass	4♡
Dble	All Pass		

Craig led the ace of diamonds, which I ruffed in the dummy. A spade to the queen lost to Craig's ace and, somewhat belatedly, he played a trump. I rose with dummy's ace, ruffed a spade, then ruffed my way back to dummy and led a trump. Had the trumps been 4–1 it would have been an expensive outing. They broke 3–2 on this occasion and a splendid +590 was in the bag.

'That was a clever way of bidding it,' said Ian, giving Nicola a shy smile. 'I'm not sure I'd have had the nerve to do that.'

'Course you would,' declared Craig. 'Automatic on a hand like that.'

'Yes, almost as automatic as a trump lead,' observed Nicola, who can be a little waspish at times. 'All the books recommend it when there's been reluctant preference to one of two long suits.'

'Looks like you might make five diamonds, too, Craig,' I added, joining in the fun. 'My queen of spades falls under the ace and you can set up a discard for your club loser.'

'Move for the next round, please!' called the tournament director.

'Enjoy your evening, Ian,' said Nicola, as our opponents rose to their feet. 'You can learn a lot, you know, playing with a good partner.'

Nicola and I shared a triumphant glance as the two men headed across the room. 'What did you mean, *reluctant* preference?' I said to her. 'My four-heart bid didn't sound that reluctant, did it?'

'Well, how can I describe it?' replied Nicola, laughing. 'You sounded as if you'd been forced to go on a dirty week-end with Craig . . . and you had to make a choice between Brighton and Worthing!'

3 A Date with Duncan

Nicola was right. After just one session at the Ruffles Club I was inundated with invitations to play – all from men, of course. I wasn't particularly flattered because the Ruffles Club is packed to the rafters with bachelors, some of them considerably less eligible than others. I played hard-to-get with most of them. Fortunately, I've never found inventing excuses difficult. 'Things are fairy hectic at work' is a good one if you're ever caught out.

I did agree to play with a guy called Duncan. He was quite good-looking in a studious sort of way and had played in some international trials a few years back. Apparently he had given up the serious stuff to concentrate on his job – something incomprehensible in the City.

Early in the evening I had to play this tricky hand:

Game all
Dealer East

	North	
	♠ A 6 5 3 2 ♡ J ♢ J 8 3 ♣ 10 9 7 2	
West ♠ 10 9 8 4 ♡ Q 9 5 4 ♢ Q 9 6 ♣ 5 3	N / W E / S	**East** ♠ 7 ♡ K 10 6 3 2 ♢ K 7 5 2 ♣ A 8 4
	♠ K Q J ♡ A 8 7 ♢ A 10 4 ♣ K Q J 6	

West	*North*	*East*	*South*
Richard Madison	Duncan	Alex Forbes	Debbie
–	–	Pass	2NT
Pass	3♡	Pass	3♠
Pass	3NT	Pass	4♠
All Pass			

I ended in four spades after a transfer auction and West led ♠10. I surveyed Duncan's hand with some satisfaction. The alternative contract of 3NT would surely fail on a heart lead, and in four spades I appeared to have ten certain tricks: five trumps, three clubs and the two red aces.

I won the trump lead in hand and cashed a second top trump. When East showed out I could see that the blockage in the trump suit might pose a problem. I cashed the last trump honour in my hand, then paused for thought.

It was no good entering dummy with a heart ruff to draw the last trump. The defenders would be able to run the heart suit when they took the club ace. No, I would have to play on clubs while there was still a trump out. The king of clubs was allowed to win and I continued with the queen of clubs. West completed the peter I had been fearing and East won with the ace.

I crossed my fingers under the table, willing East to return a red card. Not tuned into my wavelength, he played back another club, which West ruffed. I struggled manfully (as they say) for a few moments but there was no way I could avoid two losers in diamonds. I was one down.

Duncan said nothing but I sensed that he had spotted a way to make it. I leaned forward to look at the score-sheet he was filling in. 'Two pairs made the game,' I said. 'How did they do that?'

'Weak defence, probably,' replied Duncan, not too convincingly. 'Or, well, perhaps you could duck a heart after three rounds of trumps.'

I attempted an intelligent nod of the head. Duck a heart? What on earth was he talking about?

'Then you can reach dummy with a heart ruff to draw the last trump,' continued Duncan. 'The ace of hearts is still there as a stopper when you knock out the ace of clubs.'

'Don't know how I missed it,' I replied.

By good fortune I didn't become declarer again for several rounds. Then this board came up:

North–South game Dealer South	♠ K 10 4 ♡ 10 6 3 ♢ Q J 6 ♣ K Q J 3	
♠ 9 7 6 3 ♡ K Q J 9 7 4 ♢ 9 ♣ A 9	N W E S	♠ 8 5 ♡ A 8 5 2 ♢ 8 4 3 2 ♣ 8 6 2
	♠ A Q J 2 ♡ – ♢ A K 10 7 5 ♣ 10 7 5 4	

West	*North*	*East*	*South*
Anita Stokes	Duncan	Michael Stokes	Debbie
–	–	–	1♢
2♡	Dble	3♡	4♠
All Pass			

Duncan eventually passed my bid of four spades, not looking at all happy about it. Anita Stokes (who is somewhat plump for a 25-year-old . . . how on earth she managed to land Michael as a husband, I've no idea) led the king of hearts. I had to ruff, reducing myself to three trumps in each hand.

Even if the outstanding trumps were 3–3 I could not draw them before knocking out the ace of clubs. So, as with the hand I had played earlier, I decided to play on clubs before drawing trumps.

Hoping I wasn't making the same mistake twice, I led a club to the king and trumped another heart. When I played a second club Anita won with the ace and continued with a third heart. I ruffed and drew a round of trumps with my bare ace. I then crossed to dummy with a diamond and drew two more rounds of trumps. It wasn't my day. East showed out on the third round and when I played another diamond his wife ruffed and cashed two more hearts. Two down!

I looked across at Duncan, hoping for a bit of sympathy. 'I'd have made two overtricks if trumps were 3–3,' I said.

'It was difficult,' he observed. 'Perhaps you should have aimed for 650, beating the pairs who play in five of a minor.' He opened the score-sheet. 'Yes, that would have been a good score.'

It wasn't obvious to me how I might have scored 650. Not that I had any intention of denting my image further by asking him.

'How can she make 650, then?' asked Anita Stokes.

I'd never really taken to Anita before but at that moment I felt a certain warmth towards her.

'You knock out the ace of clubs and ruff the heart return, just as Debbie did,' replied Duncan. 'Then you play on the minors, hoping that if trumps are 4–2 it's the player with the long trumps who has to ruff.'

'Do you see, Anita?' I said. 'You would have to ruff, as the cards lie. Then I can ruff the heart return and draw your last two trumps with the king and 10 in dummy.'

The session soon came to an end. We were a fair bit above average but it could have been so much better, had I been in top form. Our last opponents left the table and I gave the studious figure opposite me a friendly smile. Rumour was that he treated his girl-friends to rather splendid meals. 'I enjoyed that, Duncan,' I said. 'It's always good, playing with a strong partner; you learn such a lot.'

I waited for him to make a suitable reply but he was busy adding up his estimate of our score.

'Perhaps we could do it again some time,' I added, somewhat embarrassed to be making all the running.

'What? Yes, that would be nice,' he replied. 'Actually Debbie, I'm a bit tied up for the next week or two. Things are rather hectic at work.'

Feeling just the tiniest bit foolish, I muttered a farewell and headed for the exit. Rather hectic at work . . . was that the best excuse he could think of?

4 Launch of the G-Team

I make most of my bridge phone calls from work. Otherwise, well, the cost can mount up a bit. 'We'll be round at your place at 7 o'clock, Chrissie,' I said. 'Nicola and I will bring a couple of bottles and we can have some of those great pizzas delivered.'

We had put together an all-girl team to play in various local events. I was going to partner Nicola and the other pair would be Chrissie and Victoria. They're about the same age as us. Chrissie is a fairly large girl (she has a warning sign on the door of her fridge: 'Stodge Makes Podge'). Victoria is probably the most attractive of the four of us. She has naturally wavy hair that doesn't cost her a penny and wears expensive-looking clothes.

Nicola had suggested that we call ourselves the G-Team. Not that this was desperately likely to strike fear into our opponents. For some reason men seem to think females have a genetic defect when it comes to playing bridge.

Chrissie had cleared up her bedsitter specially for our inaugural practice session. I had never seen it so tidy – not a single piece of underwear drying on the radiators.

We hadn't been playing for long when this deal arose:

Love all
Dealer South

	North	
	♠ K 8 3 ♡ J 10 6 ◇ 4 ♣ 10 8 7 6 3 2	
West ♠ Q 4 2 ♡ A 9 5 ◇ K Q 10 8 3 ♣ J 4	N W E S	**East** ♠ J 10 ♡ K Q 8 3 ◇ 9 7 6 5 ♣ Q 9 5
	♠ A 9 7 6 5 ♡ 7 4 2 ◇ A J 2 ♣ A K	
	South	

West	*North*	*East*	*South*
Victoria	Nicola	Chrissie	Debbie
–	–	–	1♠
Pass	2♠	Pass	4♠
All Pass			

Looking at the South hand in the cold light of day, I can't really imagine how I found that four-spade rebid. Anyway, Victoria led the king of diamonds and Chrissie followed with the 7. Hoping for the best, I contributed a smooth 2. I was in luck. When her king won, Victoria continued with another diamond. 'Heart away, please,' I said.

I won with the jack, discarded a second heart on the ace of diamonds, then exited with a heart. Chrissie won with the queen and switched to the jack of trumps, won in the dummy. I crossed to a club, ruffed a heart, crossed to another club, and ruffed my last heart.

At this stage dummy was down to four small clubs. East followed when I led one of these and I ruffed low. Victoria overruffed, but fortunately this was with a natural trump trick. I ruffed her diamond return and was able to draw the two outstanding trumps with my ace. Ten tricks made.

'What was this absurd seven of diamonds at trick 1?' fumed Victoria.

'We said we'd play distributional signals,' replied Chrissie.

'Not on a bloody king lead, we didn't!' exclaimed Victoria. 'How can I tell if it's safe to continue the suit?'

Chrissie, who is the placid half of the partnership, shrugged her shoulders. 'You get some bad hands for any method,' she said. 'Distributional works fine most of the time.'

Victoria was still glaring across the table and for a moment I feared our new team would suffer an early demise. 'I'm *not* going to play distributional on king leads,' she said.

'OK, not on king leads,' said Chrissie, reaching into her handbag for a pack of mints.

A hand or two later I had another game contract to play.

Game all Dealer North	♠ 7 3 ♡ 10 9 4 2 ◇ 8 6 4 ♣ A 8 6 2	
♠ 10 8 6 5 ♡ 5 ◇ J 10 7 3 2 ♣ 10 9 3	N W E S	♠ K 9 2 ♡ A Q J 6 3 ◇ 9 5 ♣ K J 5
	♠ A Q J 4 ♡ K 8 7 ◇ A K Q ♣ Q 7 4	

West	*North*	*East*	*South*
Victoria	Nicola	Chrissie	Debbie
–	Pass	1♡	Dble
Pass	2♣	Pass	2NT
Pass	3NT	All Pass	

My 2NT rebid suggested 19–21 points. Nicola raised me to a borderline game and Victoria led ♡5, East winning with the ace. Since the 5 was the lowest spot-card out, Chrissie could tell that the lead was a singleton. At trick 2 she switched to a diamond.

It was none too obvious how I might score nine tricks. Still, East presumably held most of the missing high cards; perhaps an end-play or two would be possible. I cashed my other diamonds, to get them out of the way, and on the third round Chrissie took some time over her discard, eventually throwing a heart.

I crossed to the ace of clubs and finessed the queen of spades successfully. The ace of spades failed to drop the king but when I exited with a low spade, Chrissie had to win with the bare king. These cards were still out:

	Nicola ♠ – ♡ 10 9 4 ♢ – ♣ 8 6	
Victoria ♠ 10 ♡ – ♢ J 10 ♣ 10 9	N W E S	*Chrissie* ♠ – ♡ Q J 6 ♢ – ♣ K J
	♠ J ♡ K 8 ♢ – ♣ Q 7 *Debbie*	

Chrissie delayed matters by exiting with the queen of hearts. I won with the king and cashed the jack of spades, throwing a club from dummy. Chrissie had no good discard. She actually threw a heart and when I put her in with a heart she had to concede the last trick to my queen of clubs.

'Gosh, that was clever,' exclaimed Chrissie, looking at me as if I had never made a good play in my life. 'Nothing we could do, was there?'

'Perhaps if Vickie doesn't lead a heart,' I said. 'On a diamond lead it might be more difficult.'

'As if anyone would lead a diamond from my hand!' exclaimed Victoria. 'When I have a one-count I lead partner's suit.'

I could see that Victoria was going to be the 'difficult' member of the team. Still, there was no-one else we could get. She usually played quite well, that was the most important thing.

It was nearly midnight, with the red wine and the *quatro stagioni* pizzas a distant memory, when a rather good hand came along.

East–West game
Dealer East

	North	
	♠ A 4 3 ♡ A 10 8 7 6 3 ◇ 4 ♣ J 8 4	
West ♠ J 8 2 ♡ 9 ◇ K Q 8 5 3 ♣ 10 6 5 3	N W E S	**East** ♠ Q 10 7 ♡ K 5 2 ◇ 10 7 6 2 ♣ 9 7 2
	♠ K 9 6 5 ♡ Q J 4 ◇ A J 9 ♣ A K Q	

West	*North*	*East*	*South*
Victoria	Nicola	Chrissie	Debbie
–	–	Pass	2NT
Pass	3◇	Pass	3♡
Pass	5♡	Pass	6♡
All Pass			

Victoria led the king of diamonds and Nicola put down the dummy. 'Difficult hand to bid,' she observed.

'I thought we said we would jump straight to four of a major to invite a slam,' I replied. 'You know, and go via the transfer when you just want to play a game.'

'I know, I know, that was my idea in the first place,' retorted Nicola. 'I thought I was too strong for that.'

Our discussion of the bidding at an end, I played ◇4 from dummy. Chrissie, sitting East, almost played one card, then took it back at the last moment and played the 2 instead. It occurred to me that this diamond situation was an echo of the one we had met earlier in the evening.

I won the trick with the diamond ace and ran the queen of trumps, losing to East's king. When a club came back I won with the ace and drew the outstanding trumps in two more rounds.

The only possible chance was to squeeze someone in spades and diamonds. Since I would need to be in the hand with the ◇J 9 at the crucial moment, I cashed two more rounds of trumps before returning to my hand with a club. These cards were left:

	Nicola	
	♠ A 4 3	
	♡ 7	
	◇ –	
	♣ J	
Victoria		*Chrissie*
♠ J 8 2	N	♠ Q 10 7
♡ –	W E	♡ –
◇ Q 8	S	◇ 10 7
♣ –		♣ –
	♠ K 9	
	♡ –	
	◇ J 9	
	♣ Q	
	Debbie	

On the last club Victoria threw a spade and Chrissie a second diamond. Since there were still five spades out I knew that I couldn't cash three spade tricks. I therefore needed to guess whether West had bared ◇Q or East had bared ◇10. (If West held both these cards the contract couldn't be made, of course).

I thought back to trick 1. Surely Chrissie must have swapped a high spot-card for a low one, remembering at the last minute her earlier discussion with Victoria on the matter. Yes! And if she had started with an even number of cards in the suit she would now have had only one diamond left. I would have to hope that it was the 10.

When led the jack of diamonds from my hand Victoria covered with the queen. I ruffed in the dummy and the 10 fell from Chrissie. My ◇9 was now good for the twelfth trick.

'How did you get that one right?' demanded Victoria.

I put on my most innocent expression. 'Natural brilliance, as always,' I replied.

5 Back to School

The appearance of the dreadful Ralph Meredith is truly amazing. His black, Brylcremed hair is cut short in the fashion of the 1950s and he has an absurd clipped moustache. If he wasn't such a good bridge player, everyone would laugh at him.

'Ah, Debbie and Nicola,' exclaimed Ralph, as we took our seats at his table. 'Looking as charming as ever, both of you. How are you faring tonight?'

Sometimes I wish Nicola wasn't so matter-of-fact. 'About our usual,' she replied. 'A top below.'

'Yes, well, I'm sure you know that I hold an improvers' class on Thursday evenings,' Ralph continued. 'I'm always pleased to welcome newcomers, particularly two bright young things like you and Debbie.'

Patronising old lecher, I thought. A good result or two against him wouldn't go amiss. Not that the omens were good; I had just picked up a miserable three-count.

Love all Dealer West	♠ 8 5 3 ♡ 5 2 ♢ 9 6 5 ♣ Q 9 7 6 2	
♠ 6 ♡ Q J 10 9 6 3 ♢ 8 7 4 ♣ K 4 3	N W E S	♠ J 9 7 2 ♡ 8 7 4 ♢ J 3 2 ♣ J 10 8
	♠ A K Q 10 4 ♡ A K ♢ A K Q 10 ♣ A 5	

West	*North*	*East*	*South*
Nicola	Derek Hanson	Debbie	Ralph Meredith
2♡	Pass	Pass	3♡
Pass	4♣	Pass	6♠
All Pass			

Ralph cue-bid 3♡ on the first round, no doubt intending to raise a diamond response to the seven level. When the balding Derek Hanson responded in clubs, it seemed that six spades might be the right spot.

Nicola led the queen of hearts and Ralph won with the ace. Two rounds of trumps revealed the 4–1 break and he now started to finger his small black moustache. Usually this is a bad sign – it means that he's planning something clever.

Eventually Ralph played three rounds of diamonds, nodding approvingly at the 3–3 break. He cashed the ace of clubs, followed by his remaining top heart, leaving these cards still to be played:

	Derek ♠ 8 ♡ – ◇ – ♣ Q 9 7 6	
Nicola ♠ – ♡ J 10 9 ◇ – ♣ K 4	N W E S	*Debbie* ♠ J 9 ♡ 8 ◇ – ♣ J 10
	♠ Q 10 4 ♡ – ◇ 10 ♣ 5 *Ralph*	

Ralph exited with a club and Nicola won with the king. If she played a club now, declarer would be able to win with dummy's queen and take a straightforward trump finesse. Realising this, Nicola switched to the jack of hearts. Ralph ruffed in the dummy and – with the air of a Victorian illusionist – underruffed with the 4!

The queen of clubs, on which he discarded his good diamond, left him still in the dummy. When he continued with another club my J–9 of trumps were caught by the Q–10 lying in ambush behind them. There was nothing I could do.

'Pretty ending,' observed Derek Hanson.

Ralph turned obnoxiously towards me. 'You saw the point of the underruff, Debbie?' he enquired. 'I had to shorten my trumps to match yours. Had I thrown a diamond instead, I would have had to ruff the next club; that would leave me in the wrong hand.'

'Yes,' I replied, trying to sound as disinterested as possible. Minus 980. We'd be lucky to score a single match-point.

Hanson reached for the score-sheet. 'No-one else made it,' he said.

Ralph scribbled a note of the hand on the back of his score-card. 'I might use this one for next Thursday's class,' he said. 'Seven-thirty in the club basement, if you two girls are interested.'

Annoyingly, Ralph became declarer on the next hand too. All I could hope for was that he didn't have another chance to do something clever.

Game all
Dealer South

	North	
	♠ 8 5 3 ♡ K 9 8 ◇ A K 9 4 2 ♣ J 4	
♠ 10 9 ♡ 10 6 5 3 ◇ J 10 6 3 ♣ K 9 7	N W E S	♠ J 6 2 ♡ A Q ◇ 8 5 ♣ A 10 8 6 3 2
	♠ A K Q 7 4 ♡ J 7 4 2 ◇ Q 7 ♣ Q 5	

West	*North*	*East*	*South*
Nicola	Derek Hanson	Debbie	Ralph Meredith
–	–	–	1♠
Pass	2◇	Pass	2♡
Pass	3♠	Pass	4♠
All Pass			

A club lead would have beaten the contract; a heart lead would have taken it two down. Perhaps Nicola was having an off-day, I don't know, but she chose to lead a trump. Ralph drew trumps in three rounds, then played three rounds of diamonds, discarding a club. The diamond suit broke 4–2 and one possibility now was to ruff the last diamond good and hope to reach it with a heart to the king. Ralph had a different idea. 'Small heart, please,' he said.

Nicola won with the queen and played ace and another club, forcing declarer to ruff. Ralph continued with a heart to the 9 and ace, leaving me on lead in this end position:

Derek
♠ –
♡ K
◇ 9 4
♣ –

Nicola
♠ –
♡ 10 6
◇ J
♣ –

N
W E
S

Debbie
♠ –
♡ –
◇ –
♣ 10 8 3

♠ 7
♡ J 7
◇ –
♣ –
Ralph

Ralph ruffed the club exit and Nicola was left to find a discard from the West hand. She couldn't spare the jack of diamonds, obviously, so it had to be a heart. Ralph chortled to himself in somewhat sick-making fashion. 'Throw the heart king, Derek,' he said.

With that he faced his last two cards, the J–7 of hearts. 'I'm much indebted to you for that trump lead, Nicola,' declared Ralph. 'Otherwise we'd all have been deprived of that very unusual ending.'

Some forms of deprivation are worse than others, I thought. It was a complete zero our way, needless to say, and I was hoping for a drastic change of luck as I drew my cards for the last board of the round.

North–South game
Dealer South

	North	
	♠ A Q 4 ♡ J 8 5 2 ◇ A 6 4 ♣ 8 6 3	
♠ K 6 3 2 ♡ 6 ◇ 9 7 3 ♣ A K J 10 2	N / W E / S	♠ 9 7 5 ♡ 9 4 3 ◇ K J 10 5 ♣ 9 7 5
	♠ J 10 8 ♡ A K Q 10 7 ◇ Q 8 2 ♣ Q 4	

West	*North*	*East*	*South*
Nicola	Derek Hanson	Debbie	Ralph Meredith
–	–	–	1♡
Dble	2NT	Pass	4♡
All Pass			

Nicola attacked in clubs, Ralph ruffing the third round. After three rounds of trumps he picked up the spade suit successfully. The lead was in the dummy and, although I didn't know it at the time, this was the position round the table:

	Derek ♠ – ♡ J ◇ A 6 4 ♣ –	
Nicola ♠ – ♡ – ◇ 9 7 3 ♣ 10	N / W E / S	*Debbie* ♠ – ♡ – ◇ K J 10 5 ♣ –
	♠ – ♡ 10 ◇ Q 8 2 ♣ – *Ralph*	

I wasn't looking at Ralph, but I had a nasty feeling that he was stroking his moustache again. No doubt he was trying to reconstruct the hands. Nicola hadn't shown up with very much for her take-out double and he may have thought she was a strong favourite to hold the diamond king.

It seemed that caressing the facial hair had not brought its usual inspiration. Ralph gave a resigned shrug of the shoulders and called for a small diamond. When I followed with a 5, his mood changed instantly. 'Oh well,' he said, 'laughing. 'If you insist on making it easy for me.'

He covered my 5 with the 8, Nicola winning with the 9. 'I presume you have the diamond king,' said Ralph, showing his last two cards. 'You must lead from the king or give me a ruff-and-discard.'

'Excellent,' exclaimed Hanson. 'You're on top form tonight, Ralph.'

'It was more of a problem for the defence, really,' declared Ralph. 'Debbie, here, must go in with a middle diamond to force my queen.'

Nicola was looking puzzled. 'I still don't see how you're going to make it,' she said. 'What do you do if I play a diamond?'

'Low from dummy, of course,' replied Ralph.

'Then I make my king,' I said. 'That's one down.'

A disbelieving Ralph leaned over to inspect my cards. 'You played low from a K–J–10 holding?' he exclaimed.

'I was playing Nicola for the queen,' I replied. 'If you had the queen you were bound to make the contract.'

Not bothering to hide my scorecard from Ralph's gaze, I inscribed a large 10 in the estimate column. 'Well, that's what I thought, anyway,' I said.

6 A Day in the Country

I'm not one of those girls you would describe as 'easy', but when Giles arrived in my life he took me over like a whirlwind. He had graduated in Law at Oxford and had blonde wavy hair, blue eyes, and a very forceful manner. He didn't ask whether I'd like to go to the theatre, he just said he had a couple of tickets and would pick me up at six. It was the same with dinner a couple of nights later. By the end of a splendid candle-lit meal I had agreed to spend the next Sunday with him.

'We're going to my parents' place for lunch,' he informed me, as I stepped into his open-topped Austin Healey.

'But I'm not properly dressed,' I protested. Why couldn't he have given me some warning? I'd have chosen something more impressive than faded jeans and a white blouse, I can tell you.

'You look great,' he said, patting my knee.

His parents' place was monumental, a six-bedroom mansion on the outskirts of some country village in Sussex. His father, Gerald Browne, a retired judge, ushered us into the palatial lounge. 'You really must have a glass of this, Giles,' he said. 'An unforgettable little burgundy. Piers Cartwright managed to get his hands on a couple of cases.' He gave me half a glass, almost as an afterthought, and suggested that his wife might like a bit of help in the kitchen.

Lunch was rather an ordeal, the two men discussing recent high court judgements while I made small talk with Giles's mother. An enormous thunderstorm developed as we embarked on the coffee and Mrs Browne suggested that Giles and I took them on at bridge. Our options limited by the weather, we agreed.

I felt somewhat apprehensive when Giles's father doubled me in a slam on the very first deal:

Love all
Dealer South

	North	
	♠ 8 6 3 ♡ – ♢ J 8 7 3 ♣ A K 9 8 6 3	
West ♠ 4 ♡ J 9 8 4 2 ♢ 10 9 6 5 ♣ J 4 2	N / W E / S	**East** ♠ J 10 9 7 ♡ A K Q 7 5 ♢ K Q ♣ 10 5
	♠ A K Q 5 2 ♡ 10 6 3 ♢ A 4 2 ♣ Q 7	

West	*North*	*East*	*South*
Muriel Browne	Giles	Gerald Browne	Debbie
–	–	–	1♠
Pass	2♣	2♡	2♠
3♡	4♡	Dble	6♠
Pass	Pass	Dble	All Pass

Mrs Browne led a low heart and I ruffed in the dummy. How should I play the hand? There was no point in taking two more heart ruffs. With the two minor-suit entries to my hand gone, I'd be stranded in the dummy, unable to draw trumps. No, it seemed I would need to rely on dummy's club suit.

I led a trump from dummy and the 7 appeared from Mr Browne, sitting East. I was about to win the trick when I considered what might happen if the trumps were 4–1. When I ran the club suit, after drawing three rounds of trumps, East would ruff in with his good trump. I would then be exposed to several losers in the red suits.

What if I gave up a trump trick now, instead? Yes, there would still be a trump in dummy to protect me from a second round of hearts. As long as the clubs broke 3–2, the contract would be assured.

I contributed the 2 on the first round of trumps, drawing astonished glances from around the table. Mr Browne continued with a second trump but I could now draw trumps and when the clubs broke (sigh of relief . . .) I had twelve tricks.

Giles looked at me uncertainly. 'Did you mean to duck that round of trumps, Debbie?' he asked.

'Yes, of course,' I replied. 'Only way to make it.'

Mrs Browne smiled at her husband. 'Your double rather gave it away, Gerald,' she said. 'You more or less told Debbie that the trumps were 4–1.'

Judge Browne did not accept criticism from any quarter. 'Nonsense, woman,' he snapped. 'It was a standard safety play, ducking a trump. The double made no difference at all.'

Looking somewhat red in the face, he turned to his side and poured himself another measure of brandy. He and Giles were enjoying an after-lunch cognac, a pleasure apparently not open to females. As it happens, I can't stand the stuff. I wouldn't have minded being offered one, though.

'You should have led a diamond, Muriel, that was the problem,' said Mr Browne. 'Didn't you realise it was a Lightner double? She can't make it on a diamond lead.'

Call me picky, but I don't like being referred to as 'she'. The Brownes were obviously what you might call upper-class. They were by no means lacking in money, either. I found it rather surprising that good manners seemed to be the one element missing from the equation.

'You shouldn't overcall in a suit if you don't want it led,' declared Mrs Browne. 'You've said that yourself many a time.'

A rubber or two later this deal arose:

North–South game
Dealer North

	North	
	♠ A 7 6 2 ♡ A 9 3 ◇ 3 ♣ A Q 8 5 4	
♠ J 10 9 8 5 ♡ 10 8 2 ◇ 8 5 2 ♣ J 3	N W E S	♠ 4 ♡ K Q 5 ◇ Q J 10 9 6 4 ♣ K 10 9
	♠ K Q 3 ♡ J 7 6 4 ◇ A K 7 ♣ 7 6 2	

West	*North*	*East*	*South*
Muriel Browne	Giles	Gerald Browne	Debbie
–	1♣	1◇	1♡
Pass	1♠	2◇	3NT
All Pass			

Muriel Browne gave no thought to leading a spade. Despite the experience on the earlier slam deal, an overcall by her husband was virtually a court order that the suit should be led. As for ignoring a repeated overcall, that would no doubt be regarded as a treasonable offence.

Gerald Browne overtook the ◇8 lead with the 9 and I ducked the first trick. I won the diamond continuation with the ace and finessed the queen of clubs, losing to East's king. Mr Browne removed my last diamond stopper and all now depended on my luck in the club suit. If West had started with three clubs to her partner's two all would be well; she would have to win the third round in her hand and would have no diamond to play.

When I led a second round of clubs the jack appeared from West. This was good news and I played low in the dummy, leaving Mrs Browne on lead. She switched impotently to a spade and I now had nine tricks.

Not realising anything was amiss, Mrs Browne reached for her scorepad. 'Spade lead is no better,' she observed. 'Debbie had the suit covered three times.'

Gerald Browne surveyed his wife as if she were some villain in the dock. 'Play the jack of clubs on the first round, woman!' he exclaimed. 'What on earth's the point of holding on to it? Unblock the jack and I have two entries in the suit.'

The long-suffering Mrs Browne said nothing, looking down at the table. Play the jack on the first round? The idea had never occurred to her. It might happen to work on this particular deal – must do, if Gerald said so. Still, it was poor play in the long run, surely. Second hand low, that was the rule.

We played another rubber or two, no-one seeming to enjoy it very much. After a typical Sunday-afternoon tea it was time for us to leave. Giles went upstairs to collect a few things and I was left alone for a moment in the Brownes' drawing room.

There on the sideboard was something that caused me to draw breath. It was a photo of a young man, a silver cup in one hand and a fencing sabre in the other. He had blonde wavy hair and, although it was a black-and-white photo, it seemed possible that he had blue eyes too. For a moment I thought it was Giles. No, it was an old photo of his father, Gerald.

So, a dashing, handsome Law graduate could – as the years passed – change into an arrogant old judge. Perhaps my Sunday hadn't been wasted after all . . . it was a lesson well worth learning.

7 Bridge in the Vicarage

The all-girl team we had entered in the local league was sweeping all before it. True, we were only in the lower of the two divisions; but we had won all five matches, most of them by a healthy margin. Tonight's opponents were an unknown quantity, a team captained by someone called Quentin Bucket. None of us had even heard of him.

We rang the bell and the front door was answered by a tall man in a dog-collar. 'Ah, welcome, welcome,' said the Reverend Bucket. 'Such a cold night. May I offer you a warming cup of cocoa before we start?'

We had barely recovered from the shock of having to play bridge against a priest when the first half began. We sent in Chrissie and Victoria to face the Vicar. Nicola and I would be playing a pleasant-looking elderly couple.

Game all
Dealer West

	North	
	♠ K ♡ A J 10 2 ♢ A K 6 3 ♣ A 8 6 3	
West ♠ Q J 10 9 6 2 ♡ K Q 4 ♢ 4 ♣ K J 2	N W E S	**East** ♠ 8 5 ♡ 9 8 5 3 ♢ J 10 9 2 ♣ 10 9 5
	♠ A 7 4 3 ♡ 7 6 ♢ Q 8 7 5 ♣ Q 7 4	

West	*North*	*East*	*South*
Winifred Crabbe	Nicola	Stan Crabbe	Debbie
1♠	Dble	Pass	1NT
Pass	3NT	All Pass	

The West player, introduced to us as Winifred, had an enormous bag of knitting by her side. No doubt this would be called upon the moment she became dummy. She led the queen of spades against 3NT and I won with the bare king on the table.

The opening bid marked West with the outstanding high cards, so at trick two I led the jack of hearts from dummy. West won with the king and continued her attack in spades. I ducked the second round, throwing a club from dummy, and won the third round, discarding another club.

So far, so good. I finessed ♡10 successfully and cashed the ace of hearts, throwing a club. I would now have nine tricks if the diamond suit broke 3–2. I cashed the ace and king of diamonds but West threw a club on the second round. I had lost two tricks already and these cards were still out:

	Nicola	
	♠ –	
	♡ 2	
	◇ 6 3	
	♣ A 8	
Winifred		*Stan*
♠ 9 6 2	N	♠ –
♡ –	W E	♡ 9
◇ –	S	◇ J 10
♣ K J		♣ 10 9
	♠ 7	
	♡ –	
	◇ Q 8	
	♣ Q 7	
	Debbie	

The next move wasn't difficult – I led a diamond to the queen. Feeling somewhat exultant, I watched Mrs Crabbe thumb uncertainly through her cards. When ♠2 eventually appeared, I threw her in with a spade. She could cash one more spade but then had to lead away from the king of clubs. Brilliant! I'd made it.

We had heard Chrissie and Victoria arguing a couple of times and, sure enough, they hadn't enjoyed the best of first halves. Despite the good boards we had picked up at our table we were only 3 IMPs in the lead.

We made the most of some rather tasty egg sandwiches in the interval, then Nicola and I sat down to face the vicar and his homely-looking wife, Emmeline.

Love all Dealer South	♠ A K 7 ♡ 10 7 2 ◇ K 10 9 4 ♣ K 5 2	
♠ 8 4 ♡ A Q 4 ◇ J 7 5 2 ♣ J 8 7 4	N W E S	♠ 10 9 6 5 2 ♡ 5 ◇ Q 8 3 ♣ A 10 9 6
	♠ Q J 3 ♡ K J 9 8 6 3 ◇ A 6 ♣ Q 3	

West	*North*	*East*	*South*
Debbie	Emmeline Bucket	Nicola	Reverend Bucket
–	–	–	1♡
Pass	3NT	Pass	4♡
All Pass			

I led ♠8 against four hearts and the Vicar called for dummy's ace. A trump to the jack lost to my queen and I played a second spade. On the next round of trumps Nicola discarded ♣10 and I won with the ace. It was now a simple matter to cross to Nicola's hand in clubs for a spade ruff and that was one down.

The Vicar shook his head in amazement. 'That was very sharp defence by you girls,' he said. 'I can see we'll have our work cut out in this match, Emmeline.'

'You should play on clubs,' muttered his wife, reaching for her scorecard.

'No, no, it was obvious they were threatening a ruff,' declared the Vicar. 'The only chance was to draw trumps as quickly as possible.'

His wife said nothing more but it seemed to me that she was right. Once the club link between the defenders' hands was broken, it was extremely unlikely that he would then lose three tricks in the trump suit.

I was rather annoyed in a way that she hadn't persisted in explaining what she had meant. You can't ever imagine a husband giving way like that, can you?

Near the end of the match the Vicar was faced with another tricky contract.

North–South game Dealer South	♠ A 7 5 3 ♡ K 4 2 ◇ 6 ♣ A 6 4 3 2	
♠ K Q J 10 8 ♡ A 7 ◇ 9 8 2 ♣ 10 8 5	N W E S	♠ 2 ♡ J 9 8 6 5 3 ◇ J 10 7 5 3 ♣ J
	♠ 9 6 4 ♡ Q 10 ◇ A K Q 4 ♣ K Q 9 7	

West	*North*	*East*	*South*
Debbie	Emmeline Bucket	Nicola	Reverend Bucket
–	–	–	1NT
Pass	2♣	Pass	2◇
Pass	3NT	Pass	Pass
Dble	Rdble	All Pass	

Since I was on lead, my double of 3NT seemed clear-cut. I was slightly taken aback by Mrs Bucket's redouble, but I led the king of spades and down went the dummy.

The Reverend Bucket obviously liked what he saw and I feared for a moment that he might have nine tricks on top. He ducked the first round of spades and I continued with the queen – playing my highest spade to let Nicola know that I had an entry in hearts. Nicola threw a low heart on this trick and when I continued with a third spade declarer won with the ace, Nicola throwing another heart.

The Vicar crossed the king of clubs and cashed the queen of clubs. It seemed that Nicola had read my McKenney message; I was pleased to see her discard yet another heart, retaining whatever diamond guard she might hold.

The worthy Vicar was looking somewhat less pleased at this stage. He had just noticed that the club suit was blocked and that four tricks in the suit would be his limit. He crossed to dummy's ace of clubs, then back to the high spot-card in his hand.

Nicola had kept the diamond suit guarded, so the party was now over – Bucket had to play a heart. I pounced with the ace and cashed my remaining spades to put the game one down.

The Vicar's wife muttered something under her breath. I could barely hear it, just catching the words 'fourth spade'. Of course! If he'd ducked one more spade he could have thrown the blocking club on the fourth round of spades.

'Did you say something, my dear?' enquired the Vicar.

Emmeline Bucket gave a small sigh. 'No, no,' she replied. 'You did everything you could.'

May I be spared the day when I behave like that. In the unlikely event that I ever find a man worth tying myself to for life, I certainly won't keep quiet when he throws some makeable contract out of the window.

It turned out that we had won the match by 27 IMPs – our sixth win in a row.

'Very enjoyable, indeed,' declared the Reverend Bucket, signing the result card with an old-fashioned ink pen. 'I must say, I think we all deserve a drink after a fine match like that.'

Now you're talking, I thought. I don't have a very high opinion of clerics in general but I was willing to be persuaded to the contrary.

'Emmeline!' cried the vicar. 'These young ladies here would like another cup of cocoa before they leave. Put on a saucepan of milk, will you?'

8 Battle with the Press

Harry Stockwell, a bachelor in his mid-sixties, is what you might describe as a minor bridge writer. Over the years he has picked up an endless supply of bridge clichés and he talks about the game in the same mediocre way that he writes about it.

A contract is never thin with him, no, it's always *wafer thin*. Nor does he ever hold a good hand, it's always a *powerhouse* or a *rock-crusher*. He particularly likes phrases with a military connotation – any conventions that he plays are *in the armoury*. And, of course, asking for aces is done by *wheeling out the Blackwood cannon*.

The other evening, in the club bar, Harry was recounting how two beginners had fared against him in some hopeless doubled contract. It made me feel quite unwell, listening to him. 'I wielded the axe, I need hardly add . . . fellow at the helm took the hook in trumps the wrong way, then squeezed himself in the rounded suits . . . When the smoke cleared, we'd picked up an absolute telephone number!'

I suppose that 'smoke cleared' bit was quite clever when it was first written. Nowadays you find it in every bridge magazine you pick up.

A couple of nights ago Nicola and I were playing against Harry in a pairs at the club. His partner was a shy guy called Ian, inoffensive enough but not really my type. Half-way through the first set this deal arose:

North–South game Dealer South	♠ J 9 3 ♡ 8 4 ♢ A Q J 7 3 ♣ K 6 3	
♠ K 5 ♡ 10 7 6 5 3 ♢ 10 9 5 2 ♣ Q 10	N W E S	♠ Q 10 8 4 ♡ Q 9 2 ♢ K 8 ♣ J 8 4 2
	♠ A 7 6 2 ♡ A K J ♢ 6 4 ♣ A 9 7 5	

West	*North*	*East*	*South*
Ian	Nicola	Harry	Debbie
–	–	–	1♠
Pass	2♢	Pass	2NT
Pass	3♠	Pass	3NT
All Pass			

I ended in 3NT and Ian led ♡7, second best from a bad suit. I won East's queen with the ace and surveyed the dummy contentedly. If the diamond suit came in for no losers I would have eleven tricks; I could then try to set up a twelfth trick in clubs.

All seemed to go well at first. A diamond to the queen won the second trick and I returned to the ace of clubs to repeat the diamond finesse. This time, though, the jack lost to the king. When Harry switched to a spade I played low and West's king won the trick. Another spade went to the 9 and 10 and I ducked, hoping that the suit might break 3–3. No such luck. Harry persisted with the queen of spades to my ace and West showed out, discarding a heart.

Only eight tricks were on view and the best chance for a ninth was to find the diamonds breaking. I crossed to the king of clubs and cashed the diamond ace. Once again I was out of luck, East discarding a club. I had reached the end of the road. It was no good ducking a club, the fourth trick for the defence, since West held a master diamond and East a master spade. I was one down.

I looked across at Nicola. 'Sorry,' I said. 'I think I might have made that.'

Harry leaned forward in his usual supercilious manner. 'Yes, it was a case of "no duck, no dinner",' he said. 'In fact, there were three key ducking plays in the hand.'

I did my best to look completely disinterested but Harry is not the sort to notice subtleties like that. 'You should duck the first round of diamonds, Debbie,' he said. 'Low card from your hand, low card from the dummy. Stand-out play – it almost guarantees three diamond tricks.'

'What were the other two ducking plays, then?' asked Ian.

I caught Nicola's eye. What was she doing, just sitting there? She should be putting the next board on the table.

'Well, there was my rather *bravura* duck of the diamond king,' replied Harry, looking pleased with himself. 'Then . . ' his expression changed '. . . there was young Debbie, here, ducking the first found of spades.' He shook his head disapprovingly. 'Knee-jerk play, that, Debbie. Rise with the ace and you block the spade suit; you have time to establish a ninth trick in clubs — ace, king and low towards the nine.'

Harry made a note of the hand on his score-card. 'I can probably use this hand in my column,' he said proudly.

'What column's that, then?' said Nicola mischievously. 'I don't think I've seen it. The Sunday Times, is it?'

'Er . . . no,' replied Harry. 'Felixstowe Gazette. It has quite a high circulation, actually.'

A few boards later Nicola and I were dealt a possible slam hand.

North–South game
Dealer South

	North	
	♠ A 8 6 2 ♡ J 7 4 2 ◇ K 2 ♣ Q 10 4	
West ♠ – ♡ Q 8 5 3 ◇ 10 8 6 5 3 ♣ J 9 3 2	N W E S	**East** ♠ Q 10 9 7 ♡ 10 9 6 ◇ Q J 7 ♣ K 7 5
	♠ K J 5 4 3 ♡ A K ◇ A 9 4 ♣ A 8 6	

West	*North*	*East*	*South*
Ian	Nicola	Harry	Debbie
–	–	–	2NT
Pass	3♣	Pass	3♠
Pass	4NT	Pass	5♠
Pass	6♠	All Pass	

Ian made his lead, face down, and looked across to see if his partner had any questions to ask. Harry, of course, *always* asks questions about the bidding. 'Five-card Stayman, presumably?' he said.

I sighed patiently. 'No, just ordinary Stayman,' I replied, speaking slowly as if to a child.

'And 4NT was Roman Key-Card?' he persisted.

'No, just ordinary Blackwood,' I replied.

Smiling in superior fashion at these antiquated methods, Harry indicated that Ian should face his lead. He turned over ◇8 and Nicola put down what Harry would doubtless describe as a threadbare dummy. Still, it was quite a good slam by our standards. If I could pick up the trumps, I would just have to guess right in clubs.

I won the diamond lead with the ace and played a trump. Ian discarded a diamond and looked up at me, as people do, to gauge my reaction. 'Ace, please,' I said.

With a certain trump trick to be lost, prospects were extremely poor. If the queen of hearts was tripleton perhaps I could ruff it out and discard a club on dummy's jack of hearts. I might then be able to end-play East to lead away from the club king. Nothing else suggested itself. I took the marked finesse of the jack of trumps, cashed the top two hearts, and crossed to the king of diamonds. A heart ruff failed to bring down the queen and I re-entered dummy with a diamond ruff. These cards remained:

	Nicola	
	♠ 6	
	♡ 7	
	♢ –	
	♣ Q 10 4	
Ian		*Harry*
♠ –	N	♠ Q 10
♡ Q	W E	♡ –
♢ –	S	♢ –
♣ J 9 3 2		♣ K 7 5
	♠ K 5	
	♡ –	
	♢ –	
	♣ A 8 6	
	Debbie	

I could promote my ♠5 by leading the heart but I would then have to lead away from the clubs. How about throwing East in with a trump? I decided to try that. At least I might get out for one down if he held the king of clubs.

I crossed to the king of trumps, West throwing a club, then exited with the five of trumps. West had to keep his heart guard, so he discarded another club. 'Throw the heart,' I said.

When Harry won the trump with the queen and exited with a club I played low. Ian put in the 9 and I won with the dummy's 10. A brilliant idea now occurred to me. 'Queen of clubs, please,' I said.

A subdued Harry covered with the king. I won with the ace and . . . the jack fell from West! 'That makes my eight of clubs good, doesn't it?' I said, facing the card with a small flourish.

Nicola looked exultantly at Harry. 'You see?',' she said. 'Anyone can learn fancy conventions but you don't often see card-play like that, do you?'

'Might make a good hand for the Felixstowe Wotsit,' I suggested, smiling sweetly as I gathered up my cards. 'Shall I write the hand down for you, Harry?'

Much to my delight I saw that Harry actually was making a note of the hand.

'Make sure you get it right,' declared Nicola imperiously. 'Harry Stockwell was East, remember, not South.'

9 After You, Partner

Every year the Ruffles Club and the New Acol Club do battle for the Hardiman Cup. It's an unusual event, each team consisting of four pairs: one male, one female, one mixed and one under-21.

Nicola and I were to be the ladies pair for the Ruffles Club and Ralph Meredith, captain of the team, had let it be known that our selection was against his better judgement. We were absolutely determined to do well and prove him wrong.

We played quite competently against two elderly ladies and against their mixed pair, and at half-time the Ruffles Club led by 7 IMPs. In the second half we started against their men, both internationals. I'd like to report that Nicola and I stitched them up, but in fact we had two really awful boards and didn't do that well on the other six. 'Ralph will hit the roof when he hears about that six hearts they made,' I said, as we moved for the last round.

Nicola winced. 'Yes,' she replied. 'And that double of three clubs was a disaster, too. It isn't pairs, you know.'

I was hoping for an easier ride on the last eight boards, when we faced the Acol Club's junior pair, Stuart Hornsley and Julian Dyer. Unlike the students of my day (makes me sound old . . . it was only four years ago) they were both very smartly dressed. They had impeccable haircuts, too. One guy I went out with when I was at university used to cut his own hair to save money – used a couple of mirrors for the purpose, so he told me.

I thought I defended quite well on this board:

Game all
Dealer South

	North	
	♠ 8 6 3 2 ♡ A K 7 ♢ K 10 3 ♣ 8 6 5	
♠ Q ♡ 9 6 4 ♢ J 9 4 2 ♣ K Q J 7 2	N / W E / S	♠ J 10 7 ♡ Q 10 8 5 2 ♢ Q 7 6 ♣ 10 3
	♠ A K 9 5 4 ♡ J 3 ♢ A 8 5 ♣ A 9 4	

West	*North*	*East*	*South*
Debbie	Julian Dyer	Nicola	Stuart Hornsley
–	–	–	1♠
Pass	3♠	Pass	4♠
All Pass			

The young declarer won the second round of clubs and cashed two rounds of trumps, finding he had a loser there. He then eliminated the heart suit and threw me in with a club. Sitting West, I had to find an exit in this end position:

	Julian	
	♠ 8 6 ♡ – ♢ K 10 3 ♣ –	
Debbie ♠ – ♡ – ♢ J 9 4 2 ♣ 7	N / W E / S	*Nicola* ♠ J ♡ Q ♢ Q 7 6 ♣ –
	♠ 9 5 ♡ – ♢ A 8 5 ♣ – *Stuart*	

I had to play a diamond, obviously, but *which* diamond? The 2 or the 4 would give declarer the chance to play low from dummy, easily making three diamond tricks. In some situations the jack would be good enough. Not here, though. Declarer would win in hand with the ace, then end-play partner with the last trump.

I'm pleased to tell you that I found just the right card for the occasion – the 9. The cherubic-faced declarer gave a small sigh. 'Ten, please,' he said.

He won Nicola's queen with the ace and exited with a trump, as expected. But now Nicola could lead ♢7 through his 8. He had to lose a diamond trick and that was one down.

Hornsley gave me a respectful glance. 'Good card that nine of diamonds,' he said. 'Don't think I can make it against best defence.'

'What if you throw me in with the trump first,' suggested Nicola, 'instead of throwing Debbie in with a club? Is that any good?'

The young lad considered this. 'Yes, I see,' he said eventually. 'You would have to play a low diamond to partner's jack and the dummy's king. Now I throw your partner in with a club and she has to lead from the 9.' He glanced across the table, giving an apologetic shrug of the shoulders. 'Looks like they're right, Julian,' he said.

What a charming boy, I thought. Pity he wasn't a few years older . . .

A few boards later I picked up this fateful hand:

♠ 10 ♡ 10 6 4 3 ♢ Q 10 8 7 4 ♣ A 6 4

The choirboy on my right opened one heart and his partner responded one spade. He made a game-forcing three-diamond rebid and his partner rebid three spades. Now came a surprising call by the opener. 'Seven hearts,' said Stuart Hornsley.

This was passed out. The auction had been: 1♡ – 1♠ – 3♢ – 3♠ – 7♡ and I now had to find an opening lead.

Declarer's leap to the grand marked him with a club void, so it would be fairly silly to lead the ace of clubs. A diamond lead, into a bid suit, would be even more absurd. Eventually I decided to lead a trump; you never know, there could be a ruffing value in dummy.

The full deal, which has plagued me in my nightmares ever since, was:

Game all
Dealer South

	North	
	♠ K 9 7 5 4 3 ♡ 7 ◇ K 6 3 ♣ J 9 7	
West ♠ 10 ♡ 10 6 4 3 ◇ Q 10 8 7 4 ♣ A 6 4	N / W E / S	**East** ♠ J 8 6 ♡ 8 5 2 ◇ J 9 2 ♣ K Q 10 3
	♠ A Q 2 ♡ A K Q J 9 ◇ A 5 ♣ 8 5 2	

West	*North*	*East*	*South*
Debbie	Julian Dyer	Nicola	Stuart Hornsley
–	–	–	1♡
Pass	1♠	Pass	3◇
Pass	3♠	Pass	7♡
All Pass			

Yes, the young monster in the South seat had leapt to the grand with three top club losers in his hand! He won my trump lead, drew trumps in four rounds, and cashed the ace of spades. When we both followed he claimed thirteen tricks – six spades, five hearts and two top diamonds.

'Thought we needed a good one,' said Hornsley, grinning at his partner. 'No point in bidding six. They were bound to lead the unbid suit against that.'

I may have mentioned before that Nicola tends to be somewhat less than sympathetic when a disaster arises. 'You had the ace of clubs, Debbie?' she exclaimed. 'I don't believe it! Lead a club and we take the first three tricks.'

'Trump promotion too, isn't there?' said the North player. 'Yes, after four rounds of clubs you can't even make four hearts, Stuart.'

'Four rounds of clubs would sink four spades too,' added the young declarer. 'West can uppercut with the 10 and East makes a trump trick.'

Julian Dyer chuckled to himself. 'Sort of hand Victor Mollo would have liked,' he observed. 'The only games you can make are 3NT and seven hearts.'

All too soon we had finished the set and it was time to compare scores. I looked apprehensively at the several horrors on our score-card. We had been last to finish and our team-mates were gathered around Ralph Meredith, having already handed in their scores. They looked quite pleased with themselves, and were beckoning us to join them, eager to find out how we had done.

'I'll be back in a moment, Nicola,' I said. 'Just popping to the loo.'

'Oh no, you're not,' said Nicola, blocking my path. 'If any-one's going to the loo, it'll be me. You made the wrong lead against that grand just now, you doubled the two men into game in three clubs, and you had a good half-share of that defensive cock-up against six hearts.'

Swallowing deeply, I set off across the room with Nicola in my wake. 'Thanks, pard,' I said.

10 Last Minute Substitute

Nicola had cancelled for the Thursday night pairs. Not that I minded particularly, but it is rather bad manners when you've already agreed to play with someone. So what if she'd just met a boy with a Volvo company car and his own 4-bedroomed house? Do friendships stretching back years mean nothing? Couldn't they have gone out to dinner some other night?

I turned up at the Ruffles Club anyway, intending to console myself with a lager or two and watch a few boards. 'Ah, Debbie,' said Edgbaston, the club owner. 'Fergus Masterson has been let down by his partner.'

'I know the feeling,' I replied.

'Yes, but he's asked me to find him someone to play with,' continued Edgbaston. 'Do me a favour, will you? It'll be good experience for you.'

Fergus Masterson can be accurately summed up as a card-carrying male chauvinist. He first played for England back in the fifties and has won the Gold Cup several times. Still, it was quite an exciting prospect to partner someone so famous. 'OK,' I said.

Masterson's eyes narrowed as I took the seat opposite him. No doubt he had not expected Edgbaston to produce a member of the 'weaker sex'. He pulled his pipe out of his mouth. Smoking was not allowed at the Ruffles Club but Masterson didn't regard such restrictions as applying to him. 'Strong no-trump and Blackwood all right for you?' he said.

I expect he thought anything more complicated would be beyond me. A modicum of bravado seemed in order. 'Fine, as long as it's Roman Key-Card,' I replied. 'And I like to play transfer bids opposite 1NT and 2NT.'

I passed unscathed through the first half of the session. Then, on the seventh round, we found ourselves facing one of the club's strongest pairs, Maurice Liebermann and David Elwin. This was our first board against them:

Game all
Dealer South

	North	
	♠ J 6 2 ♡ 7 4 ♢ A 8 2 ♣ 10 9 6 3 2	
West ♠ 8 5 3 ♡ A Q 2 ♢ K 7 3 ♣ A J 8 4	N W E S	**East** ♠ 9 4 ♡ K J 10 8 5 ♢ 9 6 5 4 ♣ Q 7
	♠ A K Q 10 7 ♡ 9 6 3 ♢ Q J 10 ♣ K 5	
	South	

West	*North*	*East*	*South*
Maurice Liebermann	Fergus Masterson	David Elwin	Debbie
–	–	–	1♠
Dble	2♠	3♡	3♠
All Pass			

Liebermann led a trump and down went the dummy. It was typical of him to find the most annoying opening lead. The diamond finesse was likely to succeed and on any other lead I could have brought the total to nine tricks by ruffing a heart.

Deprived of a heart ruff, I would need to make something of the club suit. The bidding marked West with the club ace but East might well hold Qx or Jx in the suit. Yes, and in that case it seemed that I could establish a club trick by leading the 10 from dummy. To make this play I would need to win the trump lead on the table. 'Jack, please,' I said.

At trick 2 I led ♣10 from the table and was pleased to see East cover with the queen. West took my king with the ace, leaving me in a strong position. If the defenders returned a trump I would be able to establish at least one discard on the clubs. And if they didn't, of course, I would be able to ruff a heart. Fergus Masterson had a very low opinion of female card-play, by all accounts. I dare say one hand wouldn't change his views on the matter, but he was bound to be impressed by my play in the club suit.

'You to play, partner,' said Fergus Masterson.

I looked up to see that Liebermann had exited with an unexpected card – the king of diamonds. The implications of this didn't take long to sink in. With my last entry to dummy extinguished, it would no longer be possible to enjoy a club trick. I went through the motions of ducking two hearts but of course the defenders switched mercilessly back to trumps each time and I finished one down.

Masterson peered over his spectacles at the scoresheet. 'Not the best,' he observed. 'Everyone else in spades managed to make nine tricks.'

'So would I, without that king of diamonds switch,' I replied, 'I don't expect anyone else found the defence.'

Fergus Masterson gave a dismissive flap of the hand. 'You used the wrong entry for the first club lead, young lady, that was the problem,' he declared. 'Use the diamond entry first, then you can reach the established club with the jack of trumps.'

'But I needed to finesse the diamonds,' I protested.

With a withering look Masterson reached for the next board. I began to understand what he meant. Had I won the trump lead in hand, I could have played on diamonds until West covered. In dummy with the ace of diamonds, I could then have made my clever play in clubs. It was a disappointing hand. I had come within inches of a real brilliancy, only to fall at the first hurdle.

A brief respite from the front line would have been welcome but on the very next hand I was declarer again.

East–West game
Dealer West

North
♠ K Q
♡ K 8 2
◇ A K 5
♣ 10 9 6 5 2

West		East
♠ A J 10 3	N	♠ 8 5
♡ Q 4	W E	♡ J 9 7
◇ Q J 10 7 2	S	◇ 9 6 4
♣ K 4		♣ Q J 8 7 3

South
♠ 9 7 6 4 2
♡ A 10 6 5 3
◇ 8 3
♣ A

West	*North*	*East*	*South*
Maurice Liebermann	Fergus Masterson	David Elwin	Debbie
1◇	1NT	Pass	2♡
Pass	2♠	Pass	3♡
Pass	3NT	Pass	4♡
All Pass			

'Three hearts was forcing?' enquired Liebermann, who was on lead.

'No idea, Maurice,' replied Masterson. 'We agreed to play transfers but the young lady and I have never played together before.'

Call me paranoid, but there was something about his tone that suggested 'and we won't play together again if I have anything to do with it.'

Liebermann could deduce from North's strong bidding in no-trumps that ◇AK would be in dummy. Rather than attack in that suit, it seemed better to lead the club king. If partner held the ace of clubs, three rounds of the suit might kill the contract immediately.

I won the club lead and played a spade, West rising with the ace. A second club went to the 10 and jack, forcing me to ruff. I crossed to the queen of spades and now needed to return to my hand to take a spade ruff. A trump to my ace seemed the best idea and when I led a third round of spades West contributed the jack. 'Ruff with the 8,' I said.

An overruff with the 9 was not exactly what I had been hoping to see. These cards were now outstanding:

	Fergus ♠ – ♡ K ♢ A K 5 ♣ 9 6 5	
Maurice ♠ 10 ♡ Q ♢ Q J 10 7 2 ♣ –	N W E S	*David* ♠ – ♡ J ♢ 9 6 4 ♣ Q 8 7
	♠ 9 7 ♡ 10 6 5 ♢ 8 3 ♣ – *Debbie*	

East returned a club, ruffed by West's queen, and a spade allowed East to score the jack of trumps. I was one down.

'That was bad luck, there,' observed Liebermann, seeming to address his sympathy more to my partner than to me.

'It would be easy on a diamond lead,' I said. 'The club lead made it very difficult.'

'You didn't think of playing the king and ace of trumps *before* taking the spade ruff?' said Masterson.

I nodded learnedly, hoping to convey the impression that I had very nearly played it this way. He continued to stare at me, however, apparently regarding this is an inadequate response. 'I was . . er . . . worried about losing control,' I said.

'If East overruffs the third spade with his natural trump trick, you're back in control,' came the reply. 'And if he doesn't overruff, you can score your two remaining small trumps by ruffing clubs.'

'Ah, yes, make the small trumps,' I said.

Masterson proffered the scoresheet, indicating with his finger the undisturbed North-South column of plus scores. 'That's how everyone else seems to have played it,' he said.

11 Journey to the Internet

There are no good duplicate games on a Tuesday night and Nicola often comes round to share a bottle of some sort and have a good chat.

'Didn't think much of that,' said Nicola, downing the remnants of some obscure Italian red she had brought with her. 'It wasn't a cheapie, you know. I paid almost three quid for it.'

'I've drunk worse,' I replied. 'That soapy taste may have come from the glasses.'

'Are you going to show me that live bridge game on the Internet, then?' said Nicola.

We walked through into what I proudly call my Computer Room, although I expect an estate agent would list it as 'bedroom 3 (small)'. I sat down and switched on the machine, getting the usual buzz from the various flashing lights. 'Right, first of all you bring up the Web Browser,' I explained to Nicola. 'Then you cut-and-paste this Internet address into . . .'

'Just show me the bridge,' said Nicola, pushing the cat off the chair next to me and sitting down. 'You know I can't stand computers.'

I brought to the screen a list of the bridge games in play worldwide. 'Look . . . *Expert Games*,' I said. 'I was watching one of those late last night. Bob Hamman was playing.'

I moved to the game marked *Club Standard*. There were two flagged as *Waiting for players*. 'If I click on this icon we can see who's waiting at each table,' I said. 'This one has three players from Los Angeles – Edith Marshall, Henry Marshall and Hubert Whitehead Jr.'

'Doesn't sound a bundle of fun,' replied Nicola. 'Try the other one.'

'This is more like it,' I exclaimed. 'Two players from Boston, Jeff Bean and Paul Glover, and one from Sweden, Ingemar Toresen.'

'Jump in there!' said Nicola, moving her chair closer to the screen.

I clicked on *Join Game*, selected *Play* rather than *Watch* and a few moments later I was partnering Paul Glover in the first rubber. Ingemar was on my left and Jeff on my right. In a brief tapped-in conversation with the hunky Paul (or so I imagined him), I had agreed to play Standard American. I was first to speak on the opening hand of the first rubber and these were my cards, displayed on the screen:

♠ A Q J 8 3 ♡ 10 8 3 ◇ A 6 ♣ 9 8 4

'Worth a go, do you think?' I said.

'With a suit like that?' exclaimed Nicola. 'Of course.'

I opened 1♠ and Paul raised me to 3♠. 'What does that mean in Standard American?' I asked Nicola. 'It's forcing, isn't it?'

'Don't ask me,' she replied. 'It was pretty silly agreeing to play Standard American if you don't understand it.'

Since I would rather be accused of an aggressive raise than stupidity in passing a forcing call, I bid a fourth spade. There was no further bidding and this proved to be the full deal:

Love all
Dealer South

North:
♠ K 7 4
♡ 9 6 2
◇ K Q 10 2
♣ K 6 5

West:
♠ 10
♡ A J 7 5
◇ J 9 7 3
♣ A J 7 2

East:
♠ 9 6 5 2
♡ K Q 4
◇ 8 5 4
♣ Q 10 3

South:
♠ A Q J 8 3
♡ 10 8 3
◇ A 6
♣ 9 8 4

West	*North*	*East*	*South*
Ingemar	Paul	Jeff	Debbie
–	–	–	1♠
Pass	3♠	Pass	4♠
All Pass			

The West player from Sweden led ◇3 and the dummy that flashed onto the screen did not make pleasant viewing. 'Three spades *was* a limit bid,' said Nicola. 'I *thought* most Americans played that nowadays.'

Nicola and I now had to play the contract (of course at that time we could see only the North-South cards on the screen). I took the free finesse in diamonds, inserting dummy's 10. This won the trick, which seemed to give me a possibility of five trump tricks, four diamonds, and maybe a tenth in clubs if the ace was onside. 'What now?' I asked Nicola. 'Unblock the ace of diamonds and play three rounds of trumps, ending in the dummy?'

'That'll be OK if trumps are 3–2,' she replied. 'Cash the ace of diamonds, then see what happens on the ace of trumps.'

Both defenders followed to the diamond ace but when I led the trump ace an ominous 10 fell from West. 'Right, play the queen,' said Nicola. 'If West does follow, you can play low from dummy and cross to the king on the third round.'

I led the queen of trumps and West discarded a small club. 'Overtake with the king,' said Nicola. 'Now cash one more diamond, throwing a heart.'

I wouldn't normally let Nicola order me around like this. She seemed to know what she was doing, though, and I'd rather lost track of what was happening. A third diamond stood up and I discarded a heart. After finessing the 8 of trumps and drawing East's last trump, it was time to lead a club to the king. Our luck was in! When I clicked the mouse on dummy's king of clubs, East followed with a small card. I discarded another loser on the fourth diamond and claimed ten tricks.

A conversation-box from Paul popped onto the screen. '*Neat play, Debbie*,' it said. '*You do play 3S as non-forcing, don't you?*'

Nicola was out of her depth at this point, thank goodness. No idea how to send these little messages back and forth. I hit a magic key or two and tapped in my reply: '*Of course . . . wanted to start with a good one!*'

A second or so later a reply came back from Paul: '*You play a great game, Debbie*'.

'Bloody cheek!' exclaimed Nicola. 'You'd have gone down if I hadn't told you how to play it.'

'Yes, but you wouldn't even have bid it,' I replied.

The score had reached Game All when I was dealt this collection:

♠ A K ♡ A J 3 ◇ A 6 4 3 ♣ K J 7 4

This start to the bidding flashed onto the screen:

West	*North*	*East*	*South*
Ingemar	Paul	Jeff	Debbie
2♡	Pass	Pass	?

The question-mark showed that it was my turn to bid. 'What do you think?' I said to Nicola. 'Two no-trumps?'

'What, with 20 points?' she replied. 'You don't want them thinking the Brits are a load of wimps, do you? Bid 3NT.'

Ingemar passed my 3NT bid and Paul, my partner, bid four hearts. Up flashed a conversation-box from Jeff, my right-hand opponent: *What does 4H mean?*'

'How does he expect me to know?' I said. 'What is it, Nicki? A transfer, or just a strong hand?

I tapped in: '*No idea – maybe a transfer*'. Hoping that it was a transfer, I rebid four spades. There was no further bidding and West led the jack of diamonds. This was the full deal:

Game all Dealer West	♠ 10 8 6 5 3 2 ♡ 7 6 2 ♢ Q ♣ Q 6 3	
♠ Q 9 4 ♡ K Q 9 8 5 4 ♢ J 10 ♣ 5 2	N W E S	♠ J 7 ♡ 10 ♢ K 9 8 7 5 2 ♣ A 10 9 8
	♠ A K ♡ A J 3 ♢ A 6 4 3 ♣ K J 7 4	

West	*North*	*East*	*South*
Ingemar	Paul	Jeff	Debbie
2♡	Pass	Pass	3NT
Pass	4♡	Pass	4♠
All Pass			

Once again, Nicola and I could see only the North-South cards at this stage. Dummy's queen of diamonds was covered by East's king and I won with the ace. 'Looks like we'll lose a trump, two hearts and a club,' I said to Nicola. 'Unless clubs are 3–3 and I can discard one of dummy's hearts, of course.'

'No hurry,' said Nicola. 'Let's have a good think and see if we can come up with anything better.'

'You can't do that on the Internet,' I told her. 'Everyone's paying for their connect time. If I stop and think for 5 minutes they probably wouldn't let me into their game again.'

'They might not let you in again if you screw up a cold four-spade contract,' retorted Nicola. 'How about trying to make all of dummy's trumps? If you can ruff three diamonds and one club, that will give you ten tricks.'

Following Nicola's plan of action, I ruffed a diamond, drew two rounds of trumps, both defenders following, and ruffed another diamond. I then led a club to the king, which won. 'Now ruff the last diamond,' said Nicola.

'Yes, yes, I know,' I said.

I ruffed my remaining diamond and this was the position around the table:

	Paul	
	♠ 10	
	♡ 7 6 2	
	◇ –	
	♣ Q 6	
Ingemar		*Jeff*
♠ Q	N	♠ –
♡ K Q 9 8	W E	♡ 10
◇ –	S	◇ 9 8
♣ 5		♣ A 10 9
	♠ –	
	♡ A J 3	
	◇ –	
	♣ J 7 4	
	Debbie	

'Queen of clubs now?' I said to Nicola.

'No, you might get the jack ruffed,' replied Nicola. 'Try a low club instead.'

There was a brief pause as Jeff considered what to do in the East seat. If he held off his ace a second time my jack would win; after a club to the queen and ace he'd have no chance of preventing dummy's last trump from scoring.

Eventually the club ace appeared from East, followed by an obvious switch to hearts. In fact it was ♡10. I moved the computer mouse towards my ace of hearts but Nicola grabbed my wrist. 'No, West must have the last trump, mustn't he?' she said. 'If you win the first heart, he'll ruff the next round of clubs and you'll lose two hearts.'

Changing tack, I played a low heart from my hand. West could not afford to overtake or he would be end-played. East's ♡10 won the trick and he played a club, which I ran to dummy's queen. Ten tricks would be easy if West were to ruff. In fact he discarded a heart but I was now able to cross to the heart ace and lead my last club to promote dummy's trump. I'd actually made the contract.

A conversation-box flashed onto the screen from Paul, my partner: '*Wow! Brilliant play, Debbie*'.

'I don't like the way this is going at all,' said Nicola. 'It was me that found the brilliancy, not you.'

'*Let's keep in touch, Debbie*' said the next conversation-box. '*You can reach me on http://www.bosbank8.optrdr.paulg*'.

Nicola was rapidly losing interest in the whole idea. 'What does that rubbish mean?' she said.

'It's Paul's address on the Internet.' I replied, 'so we can send each other messages in future.' I jotted down the address in the back of my diary. 'Looks like he's an options trader in some bank over there,' I said. 'I've really struck gold here, Nicki – perhaps he has his own yacht!'

Nicola had turned just a tad green at the gills. 'Well, I'm not going to play any more hands for you,' she said, striding back into the lounge. 'You didn't tell me it was a computer dating agency!'

12 The Charterhouse Club

It's not often I have the chance to play with Edward, so I like to make the most of it. I left work an hour early, claiming the approach of a migraine, and soaked for a good forty minutes in a bubble bath. I then put on my prize possession – a beautifully cut black cocktail dress, from some Milan designer called Pietro Rossagni. It must have cost a fortune, but I picked it up for £12.50 in an up-market charity shop.

Edward is a smart dresser and looks more like Hugh Grant than anyone else I'm ever likely to meet. He works for some mysterious finance house in the City and belongs to the exclusive Charterhouse Club, where we were due to play that evening. Putting up with leering glances from the older club members was a price well worth paying for an evening with the gorgeous Edward.

The front doorbell rang. 'Like the dress,' said Edward, as I opened the door. From behind his back he produced a small bunch of friesias, favourites of mine.

'Like the suit,' I replied, breathing in the scent of the flowers. He was still wearing his City pin-stripe. Mind you, he'd look rather splendid in anything.

We arrived in time for a pre-game dry sherry, then stepped into the oak-panelled card room. Our opponents in the first round were typical members of the club, in their sixties and very distinguished looking.

Love all
Dealer South

	North	
	♠ A 4 ♡ Q 7 3 ◇ J 10 7 6 2 ♣ Q 7 3	
♠ K Q 8 7 2 ♡ K 10 6 ◇ K 5 ♣ 8 6 5	N / W E / S	♠ J 10 9 5 3 ♡ 8 2 ◇ A 9 8 4 ♣ 10 4
	♠ 6 ♡ A J 9 5 4 ◇ Q 3 ♣ A K J 9 2	

West	*North*	*East*	*South*
Edward	Richard Melbray	Debbie	Sir Giles Howie
–	–	–	1♡
1♠	2♡	3♠	4♡
All Pass			

Sir Giles Howie, an eminent divorce lawyer, won the king of spades lead in the dummy. A trump to the jack lost to the king and Edward switched smartly to the king of diamonds, which held the trick. A second diamond to my ace allowed me to play a third diamond. Declarer chose to ruff with the 9 but Edward could now overruff, putting the game one down.

Richard Melbray stubbed out his cigarette. ‘You can make that one,’ he said.

‘Ruffing high works, does it?’ replied Sir Giles Howie. ‘The ten of hearts falls on the next round?’

‘No, no,’ said Melbray, well known as the biggest result merchant in the club. ‘You have to ruff high, then run the nine. You pin the young lady’s eight.’

‘Ah yes, silly of me,’ replied Howie heavily. ‘I might also perhaps have stood on my head and spun round a few times.’

‘That’s how I’d have played it, anyway,’ persisted Richard Melbray. ‘The obvious line is not always best.’

Edward turned towards the declarer. 'There was another chance,' he said. 'I don't know if it works. What if you play dummy's second spade at trick 2, throwing a diamond?'

Sir Giles Howie gave a small nod of the head. 'Makes more sense then Melbray's rantings,' he said, laughing. 'Yes, it would stop the promotion as the cards lie.'

A round or two later we met the only other mixed pair in the room.

North–South game
Dealer West

	North	
	♠ Q 7 3 ♡ A K 9 5 ♢ K 8 ♣ 10 8 4 2	
West ♠ 9 8 2 ♡ J 4 ♢ Q 10 9 7 6 3 2 ♣ 3	N W E S	**East** ♠ 5 ♡ Q 10 8 6 ♢ A J 5 ♣ Q J 7 6 5
	♠ A K J 10 6 4 ♡ 7 3 2 ♢ 4 ♣ A K 9	
	South	

West	*North*	*East*	*South*
Charles Fitzroy	Debbie	Laura Fitzroy	Edward
3♢	Pass	4♢	4♠
Pass	4NT	Pass	5♡
Pass	6♠	All Pass	

West led ♣3 and Edward seemed somewhat disappointed with the dummy I put down. I couldn't imagine why, mind you. Three trumps to an honour, a king and an ace-king. Even a timid bidder would raise to six on that, surely?

Laura Fitzroy, whose rings alone would have paid off my mortgage, did her best to obscure the club situation. She contributed the queen to the first trick and Edward won with the ace. After drawing trumps in three rounds he finessed ♣9, paying scant regard to East's attempt at deception. When this manoeuvre succeeded he cashed the club ace and one more trump. These cards were still out:

Debbie
♠ –
♡ A K 9
◇ K 8
♣ 10

Charles		*Laura*
♠ –	N	♠ –
♡ J 4	W E	♡ Q 10 8
◇ Q 10 9 7	S	◇ A J
♣ –		♣ Q

♠ 10 6
♡ 7 3 2
◇ 4
♣ –
Edward

If West, who had opened three diamonds, held the diamond ace, a diamond towards the king would produce a twelfth trick. Still, thought Edward, West would hardly have chosen a singleton as his opening lead if he held an ace himself. No, the ring-laden East must hold the ace of diamonds. It was a fair possibility that she held the guards in the other side suits too.

On the penultimate trump Edward threw a heart from the table. Laura Fitzroy had no card to spare. Hoping that her husband had opened on a six-card suit and might still hold a heart guard, she eventually released a heart. Edward cashed dummy's two heart honours, both defenders following, and returned to hand with a club ruff to enjoy the long heart. He lost just one diamond trick at the end.

'You *must* hold on to the hearts, Laura,' complained Charles Fitzroy. 'It's perfectly safe to bare the ace of diamonds. Edward's bound to play me for the ace.'

'No, I was fairly certain your wife held the ace,' declared Edward. 'If she throws another diamond, I just duck a diamond and set up dummy's king.'

On the next round we faced two balding men, both apparently the worse for drink.

'Aah . . . a young lady,' said George Fields, who was looking distinctly red in the face. 'A charming young lady, too.'

'Where do you find them all, Edward?' asked William Couttes-Browne. 'You must let George and me into the secret.'

Edward laughed. 'Don't mind these two, Debbie,' he said. 'Eccentric old codgers, that's what they are.'

The two old boys joined in the laughter. 'I'll have you before the committee for that,' declared Fields. 'Insulting a senior member of the club in front of a guest. What's the penalty for that nowadays, Bill? Trouser removal in the snooker lounge, do you think?'

Not before time we drew our cards for the next board.

Game all
Dealer North

West		North		East
		♠ Q 7 3 ♡ A K Q 5 ◇ 3 ♣ A J 9 8 4		
♠ K 4 ♡ 9 2 ◇ K J 10 7 6 5 2 ♣ Q 5		N W E S		♠ A J 9 5 ♡ J 10 8 6 ◇ Q 4 ♣ 10 6 2
		♠ 10 8 6 2 ♡ 7 4 3 ◇ A 9 8 ♣ K 7 3		

West	*North*	*East*	*South*
George Fields	Debbie	William C-Browne	Edward
–	1♣	Pass	1♠
3◇	3♡	Pass	3NT
Pass	4♠	All Pass	

As it happens, 3NT would have been all right. I was a bit worried I hadn't shown my spade support, though, and put Edward into four spades. West led ♡9 and Edward quickly hid a look of disappointment as I put the dummy down. 'Ace, please,' he said.

A low trump went to the 6 and king, West continuing with a second heart. The next round of trumps was won by East's jack and Edward won the diamond switch with the ace. A diamond ruff with dummy's bare queen was followed by the king and ace of clubs, the queen appearing from West. East followed to dummy's jack of clubs, leaving these cards still out:

<table>
<tr><td></td><td>Debbie
♠ –
♡ Q 5
♢ –
♣ 9 8</td><td></td></tr>
<tr><td>Fields
♠ –
♡ –
♢ K J 10 7
♣ –</td><td>N
W E
S</td><td>Couttes-Browne
♠ A 9
♡ J 10
♢ –
♣ –</td></tr>
<tr><td></td><td>♠ 10 8
♡ 7
♢ 9
♣ –
Edward</td><td></td></tr>
</table>

When a good club was led from dummy Couttes-Browne had no answer. If he discarded twice South would do the same, then promote his ♠10 with a heart lead. If instead he ruffed with the ace, declarer would simply discard his diamond loser and claim the remainder. East in fact ruffed with the 9 but Edward over-ruffed, returned to dummy with the heart queen and scored his last trump *en passant*.

'Good gracious,' exclaimed George Fields. 'Not content with insulting the two of us, he comes home with a lucky contract like that.'

William Couttes-Browne was not listening. 'Where the Devil's the club steward?' he exclaimed. 'Can't he see when a fellow's whisky glass is empty?'

Well, you can imagine what it's like playing with a partner like Edward. The evening simply flew by.

'Nice session, Debbie, you played well,' he said, as we walked down the marble steps of the Charterhouse Club. 'You don't have to go home early tonight, do you?'

'No, no,' I replied, trying not to sound too eager. 'What did you have in mind?'

'Friend of mine has a share in a bistro, not far off,' Edward replied. 'We could pop in for a quick dish or two. Bottle of champers, if you fancy it.'

Life has its moments. I slipped my arms around Edward's waist and gazed up into his eyes. Champagne wasn't the only thing I fancied at that particular moment.

'Great idea,' I said.

13 Digging for Gold

Our G-team was going great guns. We had won promotion to the top division of the local league and were lying in second place after five matches. We had also managed to reach the 3rd round of the national Gold Cup knock-out.

It was a cold, cloudy afternoon as Victoria drove us to the match, somewhere in South London. The opponents were a middle-aged bunch – you know, the sort of men who change from one pair of glasses to another as the match starts.

Neil Franklin, their captain, gave me a condescending smile as he helped me out of my coat. 'You've done well to reach the 3rd round,' he said.

What a cheek! Typical of his sort to think that young females would have no idea about bridge. We'd show them.

In the first set I had this 3NT contract to play:

East–West game
Dealer South

	North	
	♠ A 7 ♡ Q J 8 3 ♢ Q 7 6 4 ♣ A 8 2	
West ♠ J 10 5 3 ♡ 9 6 2 ♢ 8 ♣ K 10 7 5 3	N / W E / S	**East** ♠ Q 9 2 ♡ A 7 4 ♢ K 10 9 5 ♣ Q 9 6
	♠ K 8 6 4 ♡ K 10 5 ♢ A J 3 2 ♣ J 4	

West	*North*	*East*	*South*
Bryan Smith	Nicola	Neil Franklin	Debbie
–	–	–	1NT
Pass	2♣	Pass	2♠
Pass	3NT	All Pass	

The defenders played on clubs and I won the third round with dummy's ace. Even if the heart ace lay in the safe hand I would still need three tricks from the diamond suit. 'Small diamond, please,' I said.

I was over the first hurdle when my jack won this trick. I now led the king of hearts from hand. Yes! It held the trick. If West held the ace he would doubtless have hopped in with it and cashed his last two clubs. When I played another heart East took his ace and returned a heart. I had eight top tricks now; if the diamonds were 3–2, ace and another diamond would give me the contract. What if East had started with four diamonds, though?

Marking time, I cashed dummy's long heart. East spent a moment or two considering his discard on this trick, eventually throwing a spade. It seemed to me that, had East started with two or three diamonds, a spade discard would not have required any thought at all. He must have four diamonds, surely. I cashed the ace of spades, dropping the 9 from East. These cards were still out:

	Nicola ♠ 7 ♡ – ◇ Q 7 6 ♣ –	
Smith ♠ J 10 ♡ – ◇ – ♣ K 10	N W E S	*Franklin* ♠ Q ♡ – ◇ K 10 9 ♣ –
	♠ K ♡ – ◇ A 3 2 ♣ – *Debbie*	

I was fairly certain how the cards lay. I crossed to the king of spades, then led a low diamond, ducking in dummy. East won with the 9 and had to give me a ninth trick by leading away from the king of diamonds.

Neil Franklin looked at me uncertainly. 'You read the cards well, there,' he said.

I gave a casual shrug of the shoulders, hoping to look as if I made plays like that all the time.

'Which club do you come from?' he continued.

'The Ruffles Club in Kensington,' I replied.

Franklin looked at Nicola and me with new-found respect. 'A lot of strong players there,' he said. 'An old schoolfriend of mine is a member, I believe. Do you know Ralph Meredith?'

'Yes, we know Ralph,' I replied. 'He doesn't play that often nowadays. Getting a bit old for the game, really.'

We held a narrow lead after the first set and were 12 IMPs ahead at the half-time break. I never play well after eating heavily, so I restricted myself to a small plateful of smoked salmon sandwiches. I was still feeling quite sharp as the second half began.

North–South game
Dealer West

	North	
	♠ K 8 6 3 ♡ 8 ◇ K J 5 4 ♣ 9 7 5 4	
West ♠ A Q 10 9 7 5 4 ♡ J 10 9 7 ◇ 10 ♣ J	N W E S	**East** ♠ J ♡ K Q 6 5 3 2 ◇ 7 2 ♣ K Q 10 2
	South ♠ 2 ♡ A 4 ◇ A Q 9 8 6 3 ♣ A 8 6 3	

West	*North*	*East*	*South*
Derrick Grossman	Nicola	Phillip Oakes	Debbie
3♠	Pass	Pass	4◇
Pass	5◇	All Pass	

West led the jack of hearts and I won with the ace. I suppose Nicola had enough to justify her raise but it looked as if there would be no play at all for the contract.

I drew the opponents' trumps in two rounds and led a spade towards dummy. When West rose with the ace and returned another spade, I won with dummy's king and discarded a club. Only then did a thought occur to me. If West had a void or single club, I would be able to end-play him with the fourth round of spades. I ruffed a spade in hand, ruffed my last heart, and returned to the ace of clubs, the jack falling with West. I then crossed to dummy with a trump. These cards were still out:

	Nicola ♠ 8 ♡ – ♢ J ♣ 9 7 5	
Grossman ♠ Q 10 9 ♡ 10 9 ♢ – ♣ –	N W E S	*Oakes* ♠ – ♡ K Q ♢ – ♣ K Q 10
	♠ – ♡ – ♢ Q 9 8 ♣ 8 6 *Debbie*	

I led dummy's last spade and discarded a club from my hand, Grossman winning the trick. I was pleased to see that he was looking distinctly unhappy with life. When he eventually exited with a heart I faced my hand. 'I ruff in the dummy and throw the last club,' I said. 'Just the eleven.'

Grossman looked across at his partner. 'Nothing we could do, was there?' he said.

'We're only one down in five hearts,' Oakes replied. 'You shouldn't open three spades with four cards in the other major, should you?'

At the other table Chrissie had passed on the West cards and Victoria had been allowed to play in four hearts (it went 1♡ – 2♢ – 4♡ and North didn't like to risk five diamonds, vulnerable). We gained a bundle on the board and held a useful 21 IMP lead with one set to go.

A couple of boards from the end of the match a spectacular hand arose.

	North	
Love all Dealer South	♠ Q 10 9 8 ♡ A ◇ 9 7 6 5 2 ♣ A 8 4	
West ♠ 7 6 3 ♡ 5 2 ◇ J ♣ K Q J 10 9 7 3	N W E S	**East** ♠ 2 ♡ 10 9 8 6 4 ◇ K Q 10 8 3 ♣ 6 5
	♠ A K J 5 4 ♡ K Q J 7 3 ◇ A 4 ♣ 2	

West	*North*	*East*	*South*
Bryan Smith	Nicola	Neil Franklin	Debbie
–	–	–	2♠
3♣	4♣	Pass	4NT
Pass	5♠	Pass	7♠
All Pass			

My 4NT was Roman Key-Card Blackwood and Nicola's response showed two aces and the queen of trumps. I bid seven spades, expecting to be able to claim the contract the moment dummy went down. West led the king of clubs and I saw that all would be well if hearts were 4–3; I would be able to discard four diamonds from the table, then ruff a diamond.

I won the club lead in dummy and ruffed a club with the ace. I then crossed to dummy with a trump and ruffed another club high, East showing out. I drew trumps in two more rounds, finding that West had started with 10 cards in the black suits. These cards were still out:

	Nicola	
	♠ 8	
	♡ A	
	◇ 9 7 6 5 2	
	♣ –	
Smith		*Franklin*
♠ –	N	♠ –
♡ 5 2	W E	♡ 10 9 8 6 4
◇ J	S	◇ K Q
♣ Q J 10 9		♣ –
	♠ –	
	♡ K Q J 7 3	
	◇ A 4	
	♣ –	
	Debbie	

If West had started with 3–3–0–7 shape, East would hold only four hearts; I could simply unblock the heart ace and cross to my hand to cash the heart suit. It was surely two or three times more likely, however, that West had a 3–2–1–7 distribution. In that case East would hold the sole guard of both the red suits. Yes, and in that case the last spade would squeeze him. I could feel my heart pounding. 'Trump, please,' I said.

When East discarded a heart I threw a diamond from my own hand. I then cashed dummy's ace of hearts and crossed to the diamond ace to score the remaining hearts.

'Wow!' exclaimed Nicola. 'That was a . . . what do you call it?'

Looking several years older than he had done at the start of the match, Neil Franklin returned his cards to the wallet. 'A criss-cross squeeze,' he said.

We had won the match by 33 IMPs and drove back home, feeling like world champions. 'Bad luck for them having to play an all-girl team' said Chrissie, leaning forward from one of the back seats. 'Not that they seemed to realise it for a while.'

'No, did you see their faces when we arrived at the front door?' I said. 'They looked as if Santa Claus had just delivered a big Christmas present!'

14 All for Charity

I sometimes feel rather sorry for Ian. He's pleasant enough, in his late twenties, and has a good job in the computer industry. For reasons I've never been able to fathom, he can never find himself a regular girlfriend. He . . . well, he lacks a bit of *drive*, that's the problem. Reticence is not a quality that endears itself to most females.

I partnered Ian in the Charity Simultaneous pairs last week. He looked quite presentable in a white shirt and blue silk tie. There must be some girl who'd be happy with a straightforward, inoffensive type like him, I thought. Perhaps Chrissie would get on well with him.

Ian seemed quite impressed by my efforts on this hand from the third round:

Love all
Dealer South

	North	
	♠ K J 7 3 ♡ 10 4 ♢ 8 5 3 ♣ 10 8 5 2	
West ♠ 8 6 ♡ A K 8 6 3 ♢ Q 7 4 ♣ K J 9	N W E S	**East** ♠ Q 4 ♡ Q J 9 7 2 ♢ 10 9 6 2 ♣ Q 3
	♠ A 10 9 5 2 ♡ 5 ♢ A K J ♣ A 7 6 4	

West	*North*	*East*	*South*
Ronald Weiss	Ian	Judith Weiss	Debbie
–	–	–	1♠
2♡	2♠	3♡	4♠
All Pass			

With the opponents both bidding hearts, where I had a singleton, Ian's values were likely to be just where I needed them; it was obvious to go to game in spades. Ronald Weiss, the managing director of some big cosmetics company, led the ace of hearts.

'Not much for you, I'm afraid, Debbie,' said Ian, as he put down the dummy. 'I didn't like to pass with four trumps.'

See what I mean? Most men regard overbidding as the macho thing to do. They wouldn't dream of apologising for it.

I ruffed the second heart and played the king and ace of trumps, finding the suit 2–2. Hoping that I might somehow avoid having to take the diamond finesse, I exited with ace and another club. East won the second round with the queen and switched to a diamond. I went up with the ace and played another club. This time it was West who won the trick.

Ronald Weiss had no safe exit. A diamond would run into my king-jack and a heart would concede a ruff-and-discard. When he played back a diamond I was able to show my hand, claiming the remainder.

Ian gave an appreciative nod and reached for the pre-printed scoresheet, which was of the 'instant matchpoints' variety. 'Well done, Debbie,' he said. 'Plus 420 gives us 84 per cent.'

'We score just 16 per cent here?' exclaimed a disbelieving Ronald Weiss. 'The people who score this, they don't understand bridge perhaps?'

'You need to put your partner on lead to play a diamond through,' I informed Mr Weiss. 'Lead a low heart at trick 1, that's the way to get it down.'

Judith Weiss peered over her gold-rimmed spectacles. 'You didn't hear me raise the hearts, Ronnie?' she demanded. 'You didn't think that perhaps I might have the queen for my raise?'

Ronald Weiss gritted his teeth. Any employee speaking to him like that would have been dismissed instantly. With a wife, well . . . you had to tread more carefully. 'The player who would lead a low heart from my hand has not yet been born,' he replied. 'The scorers must think some declarers will misguess the trump queen.'

'Misguess the trump queen, he says,' exclaimed Mrs Weiss. 'Debbie here is a good player. When I raise you, it is obvious I will hold the missing queens.'

A round or so later we arrived at Ralph Meredith's table. It's quite incredible but whenever I play against him he seems to have the opportunity to make some clever play. Look at what he did on this board.

North–South game
Dealer East

	North	
	♠ A 8 6 3 ♡ A 4 ◇ A 9 5 2 ♣ K 5 4	
West ♠ Q 10 4 ♡ J 10 9 8 6 5 ◇ 6 3 ♣ J 3	N / W E / S	**East** ♠ J 7 ♡ 7 3 2 ◇ J 10 8 7 ♣ Q 10 8 6
	♠ K 9 5 2 ♡ K Q ◇ K Q 4 ♣ A 9 7 2	

West	*North*	*East*	*South*
Debbie	Derek Hanson	Ian	Ralph Meredith
–	–	Pass	1♣
2♡	Dble	Pass	3♠
Pass	6♠	All Pass	

Sitting and doing nothing against Ralph is usually the recipe for a poor board, so I tried the effect of a below-par weak jump overcall. This pushed them into a slam they might otherwise not have bid and I led the jack of hearts.

Ralph normally plays the cards fairly quickly. On this occasion it seemed the contract must be posing a problem or two; he spent some time considering what to do.

Eventually he won the heart lead, drew two rounds of trumps, then cashed the remaining top heart and the ace and king of both minors. These cards were left:

	Derek ♠ 8 6 ♡ – ◇ 9 5 ♣ 5	
Debbie ♠ Q ♡ 10 9 8 6 ◇ – ♣ –	N W E S	*Ian* ♠ – ♡ 2 ◇ J 10 ♣ Q 10
	♠ 9 5 ♡ – ◇ Q ♣ 9 7 *Ralph*	

Ralph now put me on lead with a trump, Ian delaying the fatal moment by throwing a heart. When I exited with a heart, Ralph discarded dummy's last club and Ian had no card to spare. He chose to throw a club as well, but Ralph ruffed the heart exit in his hand and ruffed a long club good. He was able to reach it with the queen of diamonds.

'A suicide trump squeeze,' observed Derek Hanson appreciatively. 'That was a clever move in diamonds, keeping the queen as an entry.'

Ralph gave a self-satisfied smirk. 'Not difficult, once I turned my mind to it,' he replied.

The instant scoresheet assessed our efforts as worth 3% on that particular board. We did fairly well during the rest of the evening, however, and near the end we sat down against two somewhat conceited members of the committee. Rupert 'Director!' Bleate played the first hand annoyingly well in 1NT, scoring 72% for his two overtricks.

'Disappointing,' he said. 'I thought it would be worth more than that.'

He seemed to regard 72% as below average, playing against a pair like us. You can imagine that I was seeking some sort of revenge as I picked up these cards for the last board of the round:

♠ A 10 6 4 2 ♡ 5 ◇ A J 9 ♣ 10 7 6 2

Ian opened one heart and raised my one spade response to two spades. What would you have done now on my hand?

With five trumps and two aces, I decided I was worth another go. I made a long-suit game try of three clubs and Ian raised to four clubs. My hasty retreat to four spades ended the auction and this proved to be the full deal:

North–South game
Dealer North

North:
♠ K 5 3
♡ A K 8 6 3
◇ 4
♣ J 9 5 4

West:
♠ J
♡ Q J 9 7 4
◇ K 10 6 3
♣ K Q 3

East:
♠ Q 9 8 7
♡ 10 2
◇ Q 8 7 5 2
♣ A 8

South:
♠ A 10 6 4 2
♡ 5
◇ A J 9
♣ 10 7 6 2

West	*North*	*East*	*South*
Rupert Bleate	Ian	David Collemore	Debbie
–	1♡	Pass	1♠
Pass	2♠	Pass	3♣
Pass	4♣	Pass	4♠
All Pass			

Rupert Bleate holds the club record for calling the Director (7 times in one evening). On this occasion we must have managed to avoid any slight hesitations in the bidding. He turned his mind to the opening lead, eventually selecting a low diamond. Ian's dummy was a disappointment – he should have signed off in three spades. I had three certain club losers and, seemingly, at least one loser in the trump suit.

The only chance was to take as many ruffs as possible in both hands. I won the diamond lead with the ace and cashed the two top hearts, throwing a club. I then led a third round of hearts.

David Collemore, sitting East, is a strong player. In fact, if I were feeling generous I would say he's almost as good as he thinks he is. He could see that I would make the game if I was allowed to ruff three hearts in hand; I would score three side-suit winners, the ace and the king of trumps, and a total of five ruffs. Hoping to prevent this, he ruffed the third round of hearts with the 7, overruffed by my 10.

I ruffed a diamond in dummy and led another heart. When Collemore ruffed with the 8 I discarded another club. A trump switch went to the jack and king and I took two more red-suit ruffs. When I cut loose with a club the defenders could not prevent me from scoring my last two cards – the ace and 4 of trumps, poised over East's queen. Making the spade game was worth a 92% score!

Rupert Bleate gazed at the pre-printed scoresheet in disbelief. 'What do they want me to do?' he exclaimed. 'Lead a low club?'

'Trump lead is probably good enough, isn't it?' replied Collemore. 'Anyway, normal players wouldn't bid it.'

The event was soon over and Ian and I drifted towards the bar. 'I make us about 59%,' he said. 'Sorry I made so many mistakes, we could have had a really good score. Fancy a drink?'

Typical of him to mention his mistakes. I prefer men with a bit more self-confidence. 'You shouldn't always do yourself down, Ian,' I said.

He brightened somewhat. 'Do you mean that I played OK?' he asked.

'I didn't say *that*,' I replied. 'Most men make just as many mistakes as you; they claim they've played a perfect game, that's the difference.'

I was feeling quite thirsty but the club steward was at the far end of the bar and Ian's efforts to gain his attention were proving ineffective. I leaned forward and gave the steward a small wink. 'What can I get you, Debbie?' he said, a second or two later.

'Ian's buying,' I replied. 'Give us two pints of Guinness, will you?'

15 Lords and Commoners

The Ruffles Club supplies the scorers for the annual match between the House of Lords and the House of Commons. There's nothing arduous about the duties; you just have to record the scores and put the next board on the table. Thinking that it might be rather entertaining to see some famous politicians at close quarters, I had volunteered this year. The encounter was to take place at the Savoy Hotel and, since the doorman might not appeciate what I normally wear on a Sunday, I had put on a fairly smart long dress.

There are eight players on each team and the scoring is 'duplicate rubber bridge'. The hands are pre-dealt and play continues until a rubber had been made at one or other table. Yes, it sounds a bit prehistoric but if you've ever watched proceedings at the House of Lords you wouldn't think it out of place. I once sat in their public gallery, watching a debate on rear bicycle lights. One 80-year-old suggested that the minimum size of a light should be increased to 3 inches in diameter. A learned member from the other side of the house suggested that perhaps the brightness of the light, rather than its size, should be their main concern. Amazing.

I was assigned to Table 2B, in some chandelier-lit function room, and this was an early board:

East–West game
Dealer South

	North	
	♠ J 5 ♡ 10 5 4 3 ◇ A K Q 9 ♣ 10 8 7	
West ♠ 10 9 ♡ K 9 6 ◇ J 8 6 4 ♣ K Q J 9	N / W E / S	**East** ♠ 8 7 6 4 3 ♡ A 8 ◇ 10 3 2 ♣ 5 4 3
	♠ A K Q 2 ♡ Q J 7 2 ◇ 7 5 ♣ A 6 2	

West	*North*	*East*	*South*
Keith Markham	Duke of Sethton	William White	Lord Kellaway
–	–	–	1NT
Pass	2♣	Pass	2♡
Pass	4♡	All Pass	

It is a tradition that wherever possible Labour and Conservative MPs partner each other. On this occasion West was Keith Markham, a Welsh Labour MP who actually had some pedigree as a tournament player. His partner was a Tory minister from the Home Office. The noble Lords arrived in four hearts and West opened his attack with the king of clubs.

Lord Kellaway tapped the ash off his cigar and won the club lead with the ace. The first priority was to dispose of a club loser. Kellaway played a spade to the jack (they don't call for the cards, they play them themselves as at rubber bridge) and continued with two more high spades. West ruffed the third round with the 6, overruffed by dummy's 10. Lord Kellaway now looked for a discard on the diamond suit. This time three rounds did stand up. He disposed of a club from hand, then played a trump to the queen and king. The Labour MP, sitting West, cashed one club trick and was still on lead in this end position:

	Sethton	
	♠ –	
	♡ 5 4	
	◇ 9	
	♣ 10	
Markham		*White*
♠ –	N	♠ 8 7
♡ 9	W E	♡ A
◇ J	S	◇ –
♣ J 9		♣ 5
	♠ Q	
	♡ J 7 2	
	◇ –	
	♣ –	
	Kellaway	

Markham could see that the only chance of beating the contract lay in the trump suit. He led the jack of diamonds, hoping that if partner had the trump ace he would see fit to ruff with it and return a spade. The scorer's chair, where I was sitting, was located between Lord Kellaway and William White. It seemed fairly clear-cut to me that he should ruff with the ace. Markham watched anxiously as the Home Office minister considered what to do.

William White eventually discarded a club. Declarer ruffed and played a trump, the defenders' trumps falling together. Ten tricks had been made.

'Well played, Kellaway,' declared the Duke of Sethton, a tall man with an aristocratic lack of chin. 'Had to give you game there, with 10 points facing a strong no-trump.'

I could see that Markham was battling with himself, unsure whether he should point out the defence that had been missed. Eventually his better judgement gave way. 'Difficult for you, Willie,' he said. 'If you ruff my jack of diamonds with the ace and return a spade, it's one down.'

'The jack was a master, wasn't it?' enquired William White.

'Yes,' replied Markham, 'but declarer was out of diamonds too, and . . .'

White turned towards Lord Kellaway. 'Can't have a Minister of the Crown ruffing his partner's winner, what?' he said. 'I'd be carted off to join you loonies in the Other Place!'

After a splendid lunch, to which the hard-working scorers were not invited, I found myself assigned to Table 1A. Two Conservative MPs sat East–West, with Kellaway and Sethton again North–South. This was the first board:

Game all
Dealer South

	♠ 10 9 6 2 ♡ J 2 ♢ 9 2 ♣ A K Q J 5		
♠ – ♡ K Q 10 3 ♢ Q 8 3 ♣ 9 8 7 4 3 2	N W E S	♠ Q 8 7 ♡ 9 8 6 5 4 ♢ J 10 7 5 4 ♣ –	
	♠ A K J 5 4 3 ♡ A 7 ♢ A K 6 ♣ 10 6		

West	*North*	*East*	*South*
Sir John McLeish	Duke of Sethton	Diana Rowland	Lord Kellaway
–	–	–	2♠
Pass	3♣	Pass	3♠
Pass	4NT	Pass	5♠
Pass	6♠	Dble	All Pass

Again I was sitting to the right of Lord Kellaway and could see both his hand and that of the rather attractive Tory MP, Diana Rowland. It was obvious that her double was Lightner, asking for the lead of dummy's first-bid suit.

It was obvious to me, at any rate, but the elderly Sir John McLeish had seemingly never heard of a Lightner Double. Smiling pleasantly at his partner, he led the king of hearts. Lord Kellaway won the first trick and nodded with approval as he studied the dummy. 'I think you may regret that double, Diana,' he said.

He cashed the ace of trumps, discovering that East held queen to three in the suit. Not that this posed any problem, he thought, nothing could be easier than crossing to dummy to take a trump finesse. Lord Kellaway played a club to the ace and could not believe his bad luck when Diana Rowland ruffed. She reached her partner's hand with a heart and received a second club ruff. The slam was two down doubled.

Sir John McLeish, somewhat amused at the turn of events, peered over his thick-lensed glasses. 'That was a dashing double, Diana,' he exclaimed. 'What on earth made you think it would go down.'

'It was a lead-directing double, Sir John,' replied Diana Rowland. 'A Lightner Double, you know. I wanted you to lead a club.'

'Just as well he didn't follow your advice,' declared the Duke of Sethton. 'Kellaway makes it easily on a club lead. The club ruff is the only trick you get.'

He should make it easily on a heart lead too, I thought. If Kellaway had understood the message behind the double he would have used a diamond ruff as the entry to dummy, ending with a doubled overtrick. It was quite incredible. How could people entrusted with the country's government never have heard of a Lightner Double?

Two or three hands later, with the score at Game All, Lord Kellaway arrived in another slam.

Game all
Dealer East

	North	
	♠ K 9 7 ♡ 8 5 ◇ A 9 ♣ A K 9 7 5 2	
West ♠ 8 5 3 ♡ Q 10 9 3 ◇ Q J 10 8 2 ♣ 8	N W E S	**East** ♠ Q 4 ♡ J 6 4 ◇ K 6 5 4 ♣ J 10 4 3
	♠ A J 10 6 2 ♡ A K 7 2 ◇ 7 3 ♣ Q 6	
	South	

West	*North*	*East*	*South*
Sir John McLeish	Duke of Sethton	Diana Rowland	Lord Kellaway
–	–	Pass	1♠
Pass	2♣	Pass	2♡
Pass	4NT	Pass	5♡
Pass	5NT	Pass	6◇
Dble	6♠	All Pass	

Many players would lead the singleton club from the West hand. North's 5NT had announced that North–South held all four aces and the ancient Sir John made the better lead of queen of diamonds, removing a key entry to dummy.

The first problem Lord Kellaway faced was to pick up the queen of trumps. In the House of Lords card-room he had an almost 100% record of success in this respect. He crossed to the ace of hearts and led the jack of trumps from his hand. When West failed to cover, it could safely be assumed that East held the missing queen. Kellaway put on dummy's king and led another trump, pleased to see the queen fall from East. He drew the last trump and started on the clubs, not believing his bad luck when West showed out on the second round. The diamond loser could be discarded but he eventually had to concede two heart tricks and that was one down.

Kellaway turned towards me. 'Ever seen such luck, young lady?' he said. 'I sniff out the trump queen like a bloodhound, then the clubs let me down.'

For one exhilarating second I was tempted to say, 'You old fool, it was cold if you take a heart ruff.' Call me a bastion of the establishment, though. I just smiled back at him. 'Very unlucky,' I said.

The House of Commons won the match narrowly, not that anyone seemed to care too much about the result. Not long afterwards I was driving my battered mini homewards, the windscreen wipers fighting a losing battle with the rain.

Nicola would be amazed when she heard how modest the standard of play had been. Or would she? I suppose there was no reason at all to expect politicians to make good bridge players. At least they'd all had a good time and the encounter presumably made excellent publicity for the game.

My spirits were lifted as I opened the fridge door. Yes! Almost half a bottle of that yummy Chilean chardonnay. I carried the bottle into the lounge and sank into the one comfortable chair I possess, the cat immediately jumping on my lap. With any luck there would be a good late-night film on TV.

16 The Town Crier

The phone rang. 'Hi, Debbie, it's Luke,' boomed a deep voice. 'Don't fancy a session with an expert partner tonight, do you?'

'Not really,' I replied. 'I wouldn't mind playing with you, though, if you're available.;

'Very drole,' said Luke. 'See you in the club bar about quarter to, then. We can snaffle a quick half before the off.'

Luke is tall, dark and thin. He's also (somewhat of a drawback, this) a member of the exclusive, all-male, club committee. There's no problem as far as his bridge is concerned. He bids very sensibly and puts quite a bit of effort into his cardplay.

I wasn't too pleased when he put his hand on the small of my back as we entered the bridge room. I was perfectly able to walk in a straight line without him steering me.

A round or two into the event we faced Eileen Troke and Joan Cartwright, two 'bored housewives' who escaped from their husbands one night a week. I picked up this hand against them:

♠ A 6 ♡ A Q 9 ◇ K J 8 5 3 ♣ K 10 4

I opened one diamond and the next player passed. 'One heart,' said Luke, in a voice that could be heard the other side of the room. He seems to have no control over his voice at all. It's permanently set to LOUD – must be quite embarrassing in some situations.

The sensible rebid on my hand was 2NT, but I'd heard in the bar the other night that these committee members consider it *de rigueur* to raise on three-card support. With 17 points a single raise was clearly inadequate. 'Three hearts,' I said.

A couple of cue-bids later, we arrived in six hearts. This proved to be the full deal:

East–West game
Dealer North

	North	
	♠ A 6 ♡ A Q 9 ◇ K J 8 5 3 ♣ K 10 4	
West ♠ 10 8 7 5 2 ♡ J 7 2 ◇ 4 ♣ Q 9 7 3	N / W E / S	**East** ♠ K Q 9 3 ♡ 6 4 3 ◇ 7 ♣ A J 8 6 5
	♠ J 4 ♡ K 10 8 5 ◇ A Q 10 9 6 2 ♣ 2	

West	*North*	*East*	*South*
Eileen Troke	Debbie	Joan Cartwright	Luke
–	1◇	Pass	1♡
Pass	3♡	Pass	4♣
Pass	4♠	Pass	6♡
All Pass			

West led her singleton diamond and I put down the dummy.

'Only three trumps?' boomed Luke.

Eileen Troke leaned forward, smiling politely. 'Debbie isn't deaf, you know,' she observed. 'There's no need to shout.'

I looked across at Luke. 'I thought it was the fashion among you committee members to raise on three-card support,' I said.

Luke made a heroic effort to lower his voice. 'That's when it's at the two-level,' he replied, in a strange sort of whisper. 'Not at the three-level.'

What difference did the level make? You were either likely to find the best fit by raising on three-card support or you weren't. How high you raised just depended on the strength of your hand. Still, such female logic was doubtless beyond any member of the committee.

Luke won the diamond lead with the ace and paused to assess his prospects. He would certainly need to bring in the trump suit without loss. In that case he would be able to count six diamond tricks, four hearts, and the ace of spades. Only eleven tricks.

Yes, it seemed that he would need to find the ace of clubs onside.

At trick 2 Luke led a club to the king, losing to the ace. He won the king of spades return with dummy's ace and paused for further thought. Another line occurred to him. Perhaps he could reverse the dummy, taking two club ruffs in his own hand. If trumps could then be drawn in three rounds, he would be able to throw dummy's spade loser on the diamonds. The only problem was . . . there seemed to be one too few entries to dummy. What could be done?

Luke ruffed a club in the South hand, then led ♡5, West playing low. 'Nine, please, Debbie,' he said.

When this manoeuvre succeeded he had enough entries to proceed with the dummy reversal. He ruffed a second club with the king and played his remaining trump to dummy's ace-queen. The trumps broke 3–3, by good fortune, and that gave us twelve tricks. Luke, pleased with the way he had played the hand, grinned triumphantly in my direction.

'You had six diamonds!' I exclaimed. 'Why didn't you support me? The diamond slam was cold, wasn't it? In six hearts you needed to finesse the nine of hearts *and* find the suit 3–3.'

'Pairs scoring,' replied Luke, reverting to his normal megaphone style. 'In any case I put you with four-card heart support, as I said.'

Joan Cartwright looked unhappily at her partner. 'You *must* lead a spade, Eileen,' she reprimanded. 'It goes one down, then.'

'I dare say,' said Eileen Troke, 'but when I hold a side-suit singleton against a slam I *always* lead it.' She reached into her hand-bag, looking for a handkerchief. 'In any case, if you wanted a spade lead you should have doubled his spade cue-bid.'

'I might have done,' replied her partner. 'I didn't think it would be necessary; I thought you'd lead a spade anyway.'

A round or so later we met Mr and Mrs Weiss. Judith Weiss has a reputation for being somewhat of a dragon but she's always been quite friendly towards me, for some reason. She gave me a welcoming smile as I took my seat. 'Always a different partner, Debbie,' she said. 'I was saying to Ronnie only the other day, perhaps it is time Debbie was settling down.'

Any witty reply there might have been to this evaded me. Hoping that Luke hadn't heard her comment, I reached for my cards and found this unexciting 8-count awaiting me:

♠ J 6 5 3 ♡ 10 8 3 ◇ K 8 4 2 ♣ A 4

'One spade,' yelled the town-crier opposite.

Judith Weiss passed and I had to consider how high to raise Luke's spades. The hand contained nine losers, suggesting a single raise. Luke was almost certain to hold at least five spades, though, so I couldn't really count three losers in the trump suit. Also, my two side-suit honours were an ace and a king – not a queen in sight. 'Three spades,' I said.

Luke bid a fourth spade in such a reluctant tone, I was sure we would be too high. This turned out to be the full deal:

Love all
Dealer South

	North	
	♠ J 6 5 3 ♡ 10 8 3 ◇ K 8 4 2 ♣ A 4	
West ♠ A 4 ♡ A Q 2 ◇ 10 9 7 ♣ J 9 8 5 3	N / W E / S	**East** ♠ K Q ♡ K J 7 6 5 ◇ J 6 5 3 ♣ 10 2
	♠ 10 9 8 7 2 ♡ 9 4 ◇ A Q ♣ K Q 7 6	

West	*North*	*East*	*South*
Judith Weiss	Debbie	Ronald Weiss	Luke
–	–	–	1♠
Pass	3♠	Pass	4♠
All Pass			

Mrs Weiss led ◇10 and I arranged the dummy as attractively as I could. Luke leaned forward and spread the dummy's cards further apart, as if searching for a missing king. He then won the diamond lead with the ace, cashed the queen of diamonds, and crossed to dummy's ace of clubs to throw a heart on the king of diamonds.

It seemed obvious to play on trumps now, hoping for a 2–2 break. East would have won the first trump, though, and could then have given his wife a diamond ruff with the ace. Luke thought for a while, then pointed a confident finger at the dummy. 'Play the last diamond, please,' he said.

East produced the jack of diamonds and Luke threw his remaining heart. There was nothing the defenders could do. Luke ruffed the heart switch and played on trumps. The suit proved to be 2–2 and the 19-point spade game was home.

'What a game they make here!' exclaimed Ronald Weiss. 'Lead a heart, Judith, please. We take two hearts and I play a third heart; then I win the first trump and give you a heart ruff with the ace. Two down, it is.'

'You would lead a heart from my hand?' retorted Judith Weiss. 'Ace-queen-one over the opener, I hold. You would lead a heart from that?'

Ronald Weiss marked time by scrawling an illegible 420 in the minus column of his scorecard. 'They had not bid hearts,' he said.

'They had not bid diamonds, they had not bid clubs,' continued Judith Weiss. She turned towards me. 'Can you believe this, Debbie?' she said. 'From ace-queen-one, he wants me to lead.'

'I wouldn't have found it,' I replied.

'Only a husband would have the nerve to suggest such a thing,' declared Judith Weiss. 'You may be right after all, Debbie. Perhaps it is better not to be married.'

Luke gave me a sympathetic smile which rather turned my stomach. Was finding a husband the only important thing in life? It was bad enough having to put up with my mother's probing questions every time she phoned me. One thing was certain, anyway. I'd rather live a life of celibacy than be tied to someone whose voice had a non-existent volume control.

'Have you scored it yet, Debbie?' called Luke, in a voice that would waken the dead.

'Pardon?' I said.

17 Trials and Tribulations

More in hope than in expectation, Nicola and I had applied to play in the ladies trials for the European Championships. We could hardly believe it when we were one of the twelve pairs chosen. Of course we weren't really up to the standard – not yet, anyway. No doubt they like to select one or two young pairs with an eye to the future.

The great day finally arrived. I dare say it was silly of me but I spent absolutely ages choosing what to wear. Opting eventually for a knee-length dark blue skirt and a white top, I headed my tiny car in the direction of Nicola's flat.

'Disaster, disaster!' exclaimed Nicola, as she opened the front door.

My heart sank. 'What do you mean?' I said.

'I can't find that Gucci designer scarf I was planning to wear,' replied Nicola.

I eventually forced her into my car without it and we headed for the Egmont Hotel, where the trials would take place.

'We did settle what we're doing when the multi is doubled, didn't we?' asked Nicola, as a delivery van pulled out in front of me with no warning.

I slammed on the brakes. 'Typical male driver,' I said.

'Two spades says I'm willing to go on if you have hearts,' continued Nicola. 'Two hearts shows positive support for spades.'

'That's right,' I replied. 'And a pass is neutral.'

'Wouldn't it be awful if we had some ghastly bidding cock-up when one of the selectors was watching?' said Nicola. 'Someone at the club thought that Terence Roper might be there.'

'Good God!' I exclaimed. 'I hope he doesn't watch us.'

Our first opponents in the Trials would be another relatively inexperienced pair, Judy Roach and Alex Burnham. We had only just sat down against them when, unbelievably, the tall, bald-headed, figure of Terence Roper approached our table. He sat down in a spare chair, a note-pad on his lap. Talk about pressure! This was the first deal of the week-end:

Love all
Dealer South

North
♠ A K 8 6 2
♡ 8
◇ A J 9 4 3
♣ 10 2

West
♠ 10 7 5
♡ K 10 7 6 3
◇ 7
♣ K Q 7 4

East
♠ J 9 3
♡ J 9 4 2
◇ K 6
♣ J 9 5 3

South
♠ Q 4
♡ A Q 5
◇ Q 10 8 5 2
♣ A 8 6

West	*North*	*East*	*South*
Judy	Nicola	Alex	Debbie
–	–	–	1◇
Pass	1♠	Pass	1NT
Pass	4◇	Pass	4♡
Pass	4♠	Pass	5♣
Pass	6◇	All Pass	

Judy Roach led the king of clubs and I won with the ace. I suppose a megastar like Yolande Newman would have relished the chance of playing a tricky slam with Terence Roper in attendance. I was fairly terrified, I don't mind admitting.

It seemed it would be poor play to stake everything on the trump finesse. A trump to the ace instead would give me two chances. The trump king might be singleton; failing that, I could take the heart finesse to dispose of dummy's club loser.

At trick two I played a trump to the ace. Both defenders followed but the king didn't fall. Was there anything better than the heart finesse now? If spades were 3–3 I'd be able to get both club losers away from the South hand. Still, that wasn't such a good chance as the heart finesse. 'Heart, please,' I said.

It was a sickening moment when the queen of hearts lost to Judy Roach's king. She cashed a club and I eventually lost a trump trick, putting me two down.

The frizzy-haired Alex Burnham turned towards me. 'Spades were 3–3', she observed. 'If you play on spades you can get both your clubs away.'

I wasn't going to let that go unchallenged, particularly with Roper sitting there, making notes on his pad of paper. 'I had to play with the odds, Alex,' I said. 'The chance of a 3–3 break is only 38 per cent.'

'Don't you also make it if the defender with the trump king has *four* spades?' continued Alex. 'I think you'll find that playing on spades is about a 60 per cent line.'

Until this moment I had rather liked Alex Burnham. It was only when so much was at stake that the little minx revealed her true colours. Not that the inferiority of my line was likely to have escaped Roper. I squinted briefly to my right, trying to decipher what he had written on his pad. It was no use; I couldn't make out a word. Knowing him, he probably made his notes in Latin or ancient Greek.

A few uneventful hands later Roper left the table, heading in the direction of the hotel bar. We all breathed a sigh of relief and a moment later I found myself in another awkward contract.

North–South game
Dealer North

	North	
	♠ A 3 ♡ A Q 9 7 4 2 ♢ K 5 ♣ A 10 2	
West ♠ 10 9 6 5 ♡ 10 8 5 ♢ 7 6 4 ♣ 8 5 3	N / W E / S	**East** ♠ K Q 8 7 4 ♡ K 6 ♢ Q J 10 9 2 ♣ 6
	♠ J 2 ♡ J 3 ♢ A 8 3 ♣ K Q J 9 7 4	

West	*North*	*East*	*South*
Judy	Nicola	Alex	Debbie
–	1♡	2♡	3♣
Pass	3♠	Pass	4♢
Pass	6♣	All Pass	

East's Michaels overcall showed spades and a minor. Nicola agreed clubs were a cue-bid in spades and I arrived in six clubs. Judy Roach led the ten of spades, won in the dummy, and it seemed for a moment that all would depend on the heart finesse. Then I spotted a small extra chance. If East held only one trump, I might be able to catch her in an end-play.

I drew only one round of trumps, then eliminated the diamond suit. This was the position:

Nicola
♠ 3
♡ A Q 9 7 4 2
♢ –
♣ A

Judy
♠ 9 6 5
♡ 10 8 5
♢ –
♣ 8 5

N
W E
S

Alex
♠ K Q 7 4
♡ K 6
♢ Q J
♣ –

♠ J
♡ J 3
♢ –
♣ Q J 9 7 4
Debbie

'Small spade, please,' I said.

Alex, who knew from the opening lead that I held the jack of spades, had to win the trick. Since she had started with a singleton trump she now had to lead into dummy's heart tenace or to give a ruff-and-discard. When she chose to return a spade I discarded a heart from my hand and ruffed in the dummy. Twelve tricks! I was exultant.

Nicola gave me a congratulatory smile. 'Pity Roper left the table,' she said.

Damn, yes, that was a nuisance. Had he stayed five minutes longer he would have seen something worthy of one of his columns. I scribbled a note of the hand on the back of my score-card. Perhaps I could show it to him during one of the intervals.

A few moments later, Roper resumed his seat at our table. Unless I was imagining things, there was a whiff of Highland malt in the air. Nicola and I had the better of the next few boards, then I arrived in 6NT on this deal:

	North	
Game all Dealer East	♠ A Q 7 3 ♡ K Q 9 3 ◇ K 8 4 ♣ 8 4	
West		**East**
♠ 8 5 ♡ 6 2 ◇ 10 7 2 ♣ J 10 9 5 3 2	N W E S	♠ J 9 6 2 ♡ J 10 7 5 ◇ J 9 6 5 ♣ Q
	South	
	♠ K 10 4 ♡ A 8 4 ◇ A Q 3 ♣ A K 7 6	

West	*North*	*East*	*South*
Judy	Nicola	Alex	Debbie
–	–	Pass	2NT
Pass	6NT	All Pass	

Judy led the jack of clubs against 6NT; the queen appeared from East and I won with the ace. A quick count revealed eleven tricks on top, twelve if either major broke 3–3 or the jack of spades fell doubleton.

With the club suit apparently divided 6–1, East was likely to hold more spades than West. Had the odds swung enough to finesse East for the jack of spades? I didn't think so.

I cashed the ace and king of spades, both defenders following with small cards. I then led ♠10 to the queen, West showing out. That was annoying, the finesse would have worked. What now? If hearts were 3–3 I would still be OK. And if West held Jx or 10x in hearts I might be able to cash two rounds and end-play East to lead into dummy's heart tenace. Yes, and I'd better do it quickly, before Roper left the table again. I cashed the ace and king of hearts but no honour appeared. Nor did my luck improve when I led the third top heart – West showed out.

At this stage a great idea occurred to me. I could end-play West in clubs! I played three rounds of diamonds, leaving West with nothing but clubs. This was the end position:

	Nicola ♠ 7 ♡ 9 ♢ – ♣ 8	
Judy ♠ – ♡ – ♢ – ♣ 10 9 5	N W E S	*Alex* ♠ J ♡ J ♢ J ♣ –
	♠ – ♡ – ♢ – ♣ K 7 6 *Debbie*	

I led ♣8, playing low from my hand. Judy won with the 9 and had to return a club into my K–7. It was incredible. I had made one of my best plays ever, with Terence Roper watching!

I could see him scribbling on his pad. Maybe he was actually going to use the hand. I couldn't resist speaking to him.

'Mr Roper, I was wondering if I should have finessed the ten of spades earlier,' I said.

'You might have done,' he replied, rather unhelpfully.

'Glad I didn't, in a way,' I said. 'That was rather a splendid ending.'

'Yes,' he replied. 'but if West lets dummy's eight of clubs win, East takes the last two tricks in the majors.'

Good gracious, it was true. I looked at poor Judy, who had gone quite red in the face.

'You might have played the eight of clubs from dummy at trick 1,' suggested Roper. 'Not many would think of it.'

The play would never had occurred to me in a million years but I could see what he meant. With ♣4 left in dummy, the way would be clear to play the 4 to the 7 in the end position.

'Yes,' I said. 'I was kicking myself for not doing that.'

18 The Unwelcome Visitor

As the first day of the Trials drew to a close we were faring somewhat better than I had expected — 7th out of 12. Mind you, we hadn't yet faced the megastar combination of Yolande Newman and Priscilla Keynes.

We began the second day not too badly, with a 13–7 win and two narrow losses, then – I could hardly believe it – my mother's elder brother arrived. Uncle Bernard has wayward hair, wears the same brown corduroy jacket all the time, and is completely clueless as far as bridge is concerned. How he found out we were playing in the trials, I'll never know. My mother had sworn not to tell anyone.

There had been no time to tell him of the kibitzer's code of conduct as we sat down to play our big match of the week-end, against the dreaded Newman and Keynes. Uncle Bernard drew up a chair between myself and Yolande Newman. He was sitting much too close, practically touching us both. I didn't like to say anything. I wasn't going to admit he was anything to do with me, if I could avoid it.

We were halfway through the auction on the first hand when Uncle Bernard tapped me on the shoulder. 'These bidding boxes are a good idea,' he said. 'We don't have those at our club.'

Yolande Newman drew a sharp breath and peered at him through her horn-rimmed spectacles. 'Do you mind?' she said. 'You're welcome to watch but please keep absolutely quiet.'

Uncle Bernard sat back in his chair. 'Pardon me for living,' he muttered.

This was the hand we were about to play:

North–South game
Dealer West

	North	
	♠ K 7 6 ♡ 9 5 4 2 ♢ Q ♣ A 10 8 4 3	
West ♠ J 5 ♡ K Q 10 8 6 3 ♢ J 10 ♣ J 9 6	N W E S	**East** ♠ 10 9 8 3 2 ♡ A J 7 ♢ A 9 5 ♣ Q 2
	♠ A Q 4 ♡ – ♢ K 8 7 6 4 3 2 ♣ K 7 5	

West	*North*	*East*	*South*
Debbie	Priscilla	Nicola	Yolande
2♢	Pass	3♡	4♢
Pass	5♢	All Pass	

Nicola's three-heart response to the multi was pre-emptive, to play in my suit at the three level. These antics might have posed a problem to opponents back at the Ruffles Club, but they were brushed aside by Newman and Keynes. They cruised majestically into five diamonds and I led the king of hearts.

Yolande Newman ruffed the heart lead and paused to consider her line of play. There were two unavoidable trump losers, so she needed to avoid a further loser in clubs. Unless there was a miraculous lie in that suit, the best chance was surely to squeeze West in hearts and clubs. She would need to ruff two more hearts to isolate the heart guard. Entries to dummy were scarce, Newman observed. Still, these particular opponents were only making up the numbers; no doubt they would come to her aid by playing on hearts themselves.

At trick two Newman led a trump to the 10, queen and ace. She was expecting a heart back but Nicola refused to help her, switching to a spade. Newman won with the ace and cashed a second spade, seeing the jack fall from my hand. For a squeeze to work, I would have to hold 2–6–2–3 shape. At the next trick Newman made a brilliant play. She underled her king of trumps, throwing me on lead with the jack. I could hardly open the club suit, so I played another heart. Newman ruffed in the South hand

and drew the last trump with the king. She then crossed to the queen of spades and ruffed dummy's third heart, removing Nicola's guard in the suit.

It had been hard work on Newman's part but a few winners later she had arrived at this simple end position:

	Priscilla	
	♠ –	
	♡ 9	
	◇ –	
	♣ A 10	
Debbie		*Nicola*
♠ –	N	♠ 9 8
♡ Q	W E	♡ –
◇ –	S	◇ –
♣ J 9		♣ Q
	♠ –	
	♡ –	
	◇ 6	
	♣ 7 5	
	Yolande	

Newman's last trump squeezed me. I threw a club and dummy's club combination claimed the last two tricks.

Uncle Bernard gave me a sympathetic smile. 'I could see that club discard would be fatal,' he said. 'Still, it's easier when you can see all four hands.'

You see what I mean? Absolutely clueless. I turned towards Newman, trying to be pleasant. 'Nothing we could do, was there?' I asked.

'Not really,' replied Yolande Newman. 'I suppose a trump return from your partner might stop it.'

She was right. If Nicola had played a second trump when she took the trump ace, it would have killed the end-play. It wouldn't help declarer to duck at that stage; I would still have a safe spade exit.

A couple of part scores provided a breather, then Newman arrived in another slam.

Love all
Dealer South

	North	
	♠ 9 5 3	
	♡ K J 6 4	
	◇ A Q 4	
	♣ K 9 2	
West		**East**
♠ J 10		♠ K Q 8 6 4 2
♡ 8		♡ 9 7 2
◇ 10 7 5 2		◇ 9 6 3
♣ Q 8 7 6 5 3		♣ 10
	South	
	♠ A 7	
	♡ A Q 10 5 3	
	◇ K J 8	
	♣ A J 4	

West	*North*	*East*	*South*
Debbie	Priscilla	Nicola	Yolande
–	–	–	1♡
Pass	4♣	Pass	6♡
All Pass			

'Four clubs?' I enquired.

'Flat raise to game,' replied Yolande Newman. 'No singleton or void.'

Uncle Bernard leaned forward. 'You don't play Gerber, then?' he said.

Newman closed her eyes, as if fighting to control herself. 'No, we don't play Gerber,' she replied. 'And please don't speak to us during the play, or I'll have to call the Director over.'

I led the jack of spades and Newman won with the ace. Any normal player would have drawn trumps and taken a club finesse, going down gracefully. This was not Newman's way. After drawing trumps and eliminating the diamond suit, she exited with a spade.

Nicola could not allow my 10 to win, or I would have been end-played. Realising this, she overtook with the queen of spades and continued with the king. Newman ruffed, noticing with interest that I had shown out. A count on the East hand revealed that she had started with six spades, three hearts, and at least three diamonds. There was room for no more than one club in her hand.

Newman cashed the ace of clubs, raising an eyebrow when the 10 appeared from East. A finesse of ♣9 succeeded and that was another disastrous board on our card – not that we could have done anything about it.

We held our own for the next few boards, then the remorseless Newman and Keynes bid a third slam against us.

Game all
Dealer North

	North	
	♠ 9 7 6 2 ♡ A Q 6 4 ◇ A ♣ A 10 5 4	
West ♠ Q J 8 3 ♡ – ◇ J 7 5 2 ♣ 9 8 7 3 2	N / W E / S	**East** ♠ 10 ♡ J 10 8 3 ◇ Q 9 8 4 ♣ K Q J 6
	♠ A K 5 4 ♡ K 9 7 5 2 ◇ K 10 6 3 ♣ –	

West	*North*	*East*	*South*
Debbie	Priscilla	Nicola	Yolande
–	1♣	Pass	1♡
Pass	3♡	Pass	6♡
All Pass			

It doesn't take them long to bid a slam, as you will have gathered. I led ♣8 and Newman peered at the dummy through her horn-rimmed spectacles. If trumps were no worse than 3–1 it should be possible to reverse the dummy, ruffing three clubs in hand. 'Play low,' she said.

Newman ruffed in the South hand and led a trump to the ace. When I showed out the contract had become awkward. Declarer would have to aim for seven trump tricks, in addition to her five top winners outside. Newman led a spade to the ace, then returned to dummy with the ace of diamonds. 'Small spade,' she said.

It would do Nicola no good to ruff a loser with a natural trump trick. She discarded a diamond and Newman scored her second spade trick. The king of diamonds was followed by a diamond ruff, then a spade was discarded on the club ace. A club ruff, followed by a diamond ruffed with the queen, left this end position:

	Priscilla ♠ 9 ♡ 6 ♢ – ♣ 10	
Debbie ♠ Q J ♡ – ♢ – ♣ 9	N W E S	*Nicola* ♠ – ♡ J 10 8 ♢ – ♣ –
	♠ 5 ♡ K 9 ♢ – ♣ – *Yolande*	

Newman showed her cards to Nicola. 'I'm leading the club,' she said. 'If you ruff high I discard the spade.'

We returned our cards resignedly to the wallet. It was desperately unlucky that three critical hands had come Newman's way just when she happened to be playing against us.

Priscilla Keynes gave the score-sheet a disparaging look. 'One pair stopped in game, the other two went down in the slam,' she said. 'It would be six hearts made around the room in a men's trials.'

'Yes, it wasn't a difficult one to reach,' said Uncle Bernard. 'Bill Maddocks and I would have got to it. It's a good one for our version of Rolling Gerber.'

We soon finished our match and Uncle Bernard drifted off to watch the last board or two at another table.

Newman turned her horn-rimmed spectacles in my direction. 'Was that dreadful man with you?' she demanded.

I looked back innocently. 'No,' I replied. 'I thought he must be your husband.'

19 A Table at the *Piccolo Mondo*

I first met Mario at a local health club, one Sunday morning. He was six-foot tall, with an athletic build and what you might call Mediterranean good looks. We were sitting in the jacuzzi, chatting about this and that, when he found out I was a keen bridge player. A few moments later he was suggesting that we should have a game together.

'Yes, yes, it is an excellent idea,' he said. 'My uncles are both good players. We will play against them.'

I'd only just met the guy, so I had to step carefully. 'You don't play duplicate, then?' I said. 'I was thinking we could have a game together at the Ruffles Club.'

He smiled at this question. 'Not possible for me,' he replied. 'I am waiter at my uncles' restaurant. Seven till twelve every night I must work – just the same time most players are at the bridge club.'

'When do you play, then?' I asked.

'After the restaurant is closed,' Mario replied. 'Just after midnight – the best time of day. We play for two, three, hours, then sleep late in the morning.'

Not everyone could afford that luxury, I thought. Still, this Mario was a good-looking guy; it would be a pity not to take things a little further. 'All right, then,' I said.

Mario was delighted. 'Friday night, why not?' he said. 'You give me your address, I pick you up at midnight in my Uncle Giorgio's car.'

Late the following Friday, I arrived with Mario at the restaurant. The aroma of Italian cooking hung delightfully in the air as we were welcomed by two middle-aged men, presumably the uncles that Mario had mentioned.

'Ah, this must be the beautiful Debbie!' exclaimed one of them. 'You are welcome to the *Piccolo Mondo*. What you like before we start . . . capuccino, a slice of our famous *tiramisu*?'

The game started and Mario played the first hand competently to put us one game ahead. Then his uncles arrived in a slam:

East–West game
Dealer South

	North	
	♠ K 10 4 ♡ A K 2 ◇ K 7 6 4 ♣ Q J 8	
West ♠ 6 ♡ J 10 9 7 6 ◇ J 10 9 3 ♣ K 7 5	N W E S	**East** ♠ 9 8 2 ♡ 4 3 ◇ A 8 5 ♣ 10 9 6 3 2
	♠ A Q J 7 5 3 ♡ Q 8 5 ◇ Q 2 ♣ A 4	

West	*North*	*East*	*South*
Debbie	Giorgio	Mario	Arturo
–	–	–	1♠
Pass	2◇	Pass	3♠
Pass	4♡	Pass	5♣
Pass	6♠	All Pass	

I led the jack of hearts and the silver-haired Arturo won in hand with the queen. He drew trumps in three rounds then led a low diamond from dummy. Mario played small, the queen won the trick, and I followed with the 3.

Declarer now led a second round of diamonds. I played the 9 and this card won the trick. My heart exit was taken in the dummy and, unfortunately for us, a third round of diamonds brought down Mario's ace. Dummy's king of diamonds was good for a discard of declarer's losing club and the slam was in the bag.

It was an annoying hand. If only Mario could have won the second round of diamonds, a club switch would have put declarer to a guess. He'd have had to decide whether to finesse in clubs before he knew if the ace of diamonds could be ruffed down. In fact, wait a moment . . . if I'd played a higher diamond on the first round, Mario could have won the second round with the 8. Yes, then he could have played a club. I always see these things too late. Still, at least no-one else seemed to have noticed it.

Giorgio caught his partner's eye. '*Mario aveva asso-otto-cinque*, he said. '*Se Debbie si libera del nove, Mario puo vincere il secondo turno*.'

Arturo smiled back, nodding his agreement. I don't understand a word of Italian but it seemed possible that my small slip had not gone undetected.

A hand or two later the uncles had a chance to win the first rubber.

East–West game
Dealer North

	North	
	♠ 9 2 ♡ K 6 3 2 ◇ A Q 7 6 2 ♣ 8 3	
West ♠ J 5 ♡ 10 4 ◇ K 9 8 3 ♣ Q J 10 9 5	N W E S	**East** ♠ K Q 8 6 3 ♡ Q J 8 7 ◇ 5 4 ♣ 6 2
	♠ A 10 7 4 ♡ A 9 5 ◇ J 10 ♣ A K 7 4	
	South	

West	*North*	*East*	*South*
Debbie	Giorgio	Mario	Arturo
–	Pass	Pass	1NT
Pass	3NT	All Pass	

Arturo opened 1NT (strong, of course) and was raised directly to game. I led the queen of clubs, won by declarer's ace, and the jack of diamonds now appeared. I covered with the king and Arturo reached towards dummy's diamond suit. I was expecting him to win with the ace but he actually played the 2, leaving me on lead.

I cleared the club suit but Arturo now cashed ◇10 and crossed to the king of hearts to score the remaining diamonds. Four diamond tricks and five winners outside brought his total to nine.

Arturo had played the hand well. Had he won my king of diamonds with the ace he'd have made only three diamond tricks, not enough for the contract.

'Is it better if I don't cover the diamond?' I asked.

'No, no, Debbie,' replied Arturo. 'If the jack is winning the first round, I play 10 to the queen next. Still I make four diamond tricks.'

Mario leaned forward. 'On the second round you cover the 10 with the queen?' he queried. 'That loses the game if I start with king-and-one.'

'Oh, so now you are so clever you duck with king-and-one?' said Arturo, giving Mario a playful pat on the cheek. 'Your name is Garozzo, hah?'

Giorgio, the uncle to my left, rose to his feet. 'Now, I have a splendid *grappa* for you to try, Debbie,' he said.

Most liqueurs taste awful, in my opinion, but it wouldn't have been very friendly to refuse. 'Sounds good,' I replied.

A few moments later Giorgio returned with four small glasses of colourless liquid. 'Something a little special here,' he announced. He tapped the side of his nose. 'Not for the customers, you understand.'

I steeled myself as I took a small sip. It was as ghastly as I had feared . . . even a cheap after-shave couldn't have tasted worse. I managed a brave smile. 'Delicious,' I said.

Mario looked concerned. 'You don't like it?' he said. 'Please, no need to finish if you don't like.'

'No, it's great,' I said.

I need hardly say I was enjoying this late-night session immensely – it's not often a girl is surrounded by three attentive males. A glance at my watch showed it was nearly three in the morning as we embarked on this deal:

North–South game
Dealer West

	North	
	♠ K 9 ♡ K 9 3 2 ♢ A Q 4 ♣ 8 6 3 2	
West ♠ 4 ♡ J 8 7 ♢ K J 10 9 7 3 ♣ Q 9 5	N W E S	**East** ♠ 10 6 5 3 ♡ Q 10 6 4 ♢ 6 2 ♣ J 10 4
	♠ A Q J 8 7 2 ♡ A 5 ♢ 8 5 ♣ A K 7	

West	*North*	*East*	*South*
Debbie	Giorgio	Mario	Arturo
3♢	Pass	Pass	4♠
Pass	4NT	Pass	5♣
Pass	5♢	Pass	6♣
Pass	7♠	All Pass	

It was not at all obvious what to lead from my hand. To mark time, I decided to ask about the bidding. 'Four no-trumps was Blackwood, was it?' I said.

'In the *Ristorante Piccolo Mondo*?' exclaimed Arturo. 'No, no, it was *Roman* Blackwood, of course, asking for the key cards.'

'Five-club show three key cards,' said Giorgio. 'My five-diamond ask for trump queen, six-club say "yes" and also club king.'

They claimed never to have played tournament bridge? It was hard to believe.

What could I lead against the grand? I certainly wasn't going to lead the singleton trump but the other suits seemed dangerous too. Eventually I led the jack of diamonds and dummy went down with the ace-queen sitting over me. Arturo finessed dummy's queen successfully and proceeded to draw trumps in four rounds.

The best line was by no means obvious and the Italian stroked his somewhat unkempt moustache, deep in thought. If East held four or more clubs, a double squeeze around hearts should be possible. West would have to hold the diamonds, East the clubs; neither defender would be able to retain a heart guard.

Eventually Arturo spotted a better line – a double squeeze with clubs as the pivot suit. He cashed the top two hearts and ruffed a heart, removing my guard in the suit. These cards remained:

	Giorgio	
	♠ –	
	♡ 9	
	◇ A 4	
	♣ 8 6	
Debbie		*Mario*
♠ –	N	♠ –
♡ –	W E	♡ Q
◇ K 10	S	◇ 6
♣ Q 9 5		♣ J 10 4
	♠ 8	
	♡ –	
	◇ 8	
	♣ A K 7	
	Arturo	

When Arturo cashed his last trump I had to discard a club in order to retain my diamond guard. A club was thrown from the table and Mario delayed the fatal moment by discarding his last diamond. Now came a diamond to the ace. To keep his heart guard, Mario had to release a club.

'My clubs are good, I think,' declared Arturo, facing his last three cards.

'Bravo, bravo!' exclaimed Giorgio. 'What a play to find!'

The last rubber of the evening was over. I gazed incredulously at the two uncles as the cards were gathered up. 'You're really good players, you two,' I said. 'You should close the restaurant for a few days and enter some big duplicate tournament. You'd do really well, I'm sure.'

Giorgio laughed at this suggestion. 'You think it would be more fun than our game tonight, Debbie?' he said.

'More enjoyable than four good friends playing together?' added Arturo.

Mario had retrieved my coat and was waiting to wrap it around me. I looked into his smiling eyes, recalling what a wonderful night it had been. 'I rather think your uncles are right,' I said.

20 A Different Planet

On Saturday mornings I sleep on for as long as Nature intends. It was almost 11 o'clock as I slipped into my dressing gown and wandered down the hallway to see if there was any post. Two items. There was a postcard of a Seychelles beach scene. Without turning it over, I knew it was from Helen at work – typical of her to make sure that everyone knows where she has been. There was also a white envelope with an Aylesbury postmark on it.

I read the contents in some disbelief. The Polish Ladies team had been invited to attend the Brighton Summer Congress and on the Wednesday there would be a 40-board friendly match against a British Ladies team. 'Nicola Cartwright and yourself have been selected to play in this match,' the letter said. 'Your team-mates will be Pat Draper and Judy Sharman.'

For a moment I thought it might be some cruel practical joke. But then I recalled our finishing position of 9th out of 12 in the European trials. Not too bad – three pairs had come below us. The selectors had been impressed, obviously.

Anyway, to cut a long story short, a few weeks later Nicola and I were installed in Brighton's Metropole Hotel. We regaled ourselves in our finery – I had bought a new dress specially – and headed for the room where the match would be played.

We met Pat and Judy, who had played for England many times before. They were friendly enough but I had the feeling they weren't exactly overjoyed at the team-mates they had been given.

I had half-hoped there would be a big crowd watching the match. In fact there were only two spectators at our table as we started to play. This was the very first board:

North–South game
Dealer South

	North	
	♠ Q 8 3 ♡ J 6 4 ♢ A K 9 7 3 ♣ 7 4	
West ♠ K 10 4 ♡ 10 8 3 ♢ J 8 5 2 ♣ K 9 6	N / W E / S	**East** ♠ A 9 ♡ Q 9 7 ♢ 10 ♣ A J 10 8 5 3 2
	♠ J 7 6 5 2 ♡ A K 5 2 ♢ Q 6 4 ♣ Q	

West	*North*	*East*	*South*
Maria Frycz	Nicola	Irene Pukowska	Debbie
–	–	–	1♠
Pass	2♢	3♣	Pass
Pass	3♠	Pass	4♠
All Pass			

My fourth spade was rather borderline, but the Qxx in partner's suit suggested the two hands would fit well. Maria Frycz, who had short-cropped bleached hair, led a low club to East's ace. I ruffed the club continuation and paused to consider how the trump suit might lie. Since East held long clubs she was likely to have the shorter trump holding – perhaps Ax or Kx. I would have liked to lead the first round of trumps from dummy, but crossing to a diamond would risk a defensive ruff if that suit were 4–1. Anyway, if East did hold honour doubleton it would be good enough to lead the jack from hand.

When I led the jack of spades West won with the king. Sensing that I was in difficulties in the trump suit, she played a third round of clubs, giving a deliberate ruff-and-discard. I had to ruff this in my own hand, otherwise her 10 of trumps would have been promoted. When I ducked a trump I was relieved to find that this did bring the ace from East. Irene Pukowska, sitting East, was on lead in this end position:

	Nicola ♠ Q ♡ J 6 ◇ A K 9 7 3 ♣ –	
Maria ♠ 10 ♡ 10 8 3 ◇ J 8 5 2 ♣ –	N W E S	*Irene* ♠ – ♡ Q 9 7 ◇ 10 ♣ 10 8 5 3
	♠ 7 ♡ A K 5 2 ◇ Q 6 4 ♣ – *Debbie*	

She tried yet another club and I ruffed in hand with the 7. West declined to overruff, so I crossed to dummy's ace of diamonds to draw the last trump. On this trick East produced ◇10. Everything was going swimmingly well. After drawing West's trump I returned to the queen of diamonds and picked up the rest of the suit by finessing the 9. I'd made it!

The smartly dressed East player gave me a respectful nod. 'You are in the team for the European Championship?' she enquired.

'Er . . . no,' I replied. 'We did play in the trials but we just missed out.'

Pat Draper and Judy Sharman looked distinctly apprehensive as we rejoined them for the first comparison. 'How did you get on?' asked Judy Sharman. 'Any disasters?'

'No,' replied Nicola. 'Why, did you have a disaster, then?'

'Of course not,' said Sharman. 'Anyway, minus 140 on the first one.'

'Plus 620,' I said.

I felt great. I could really get hooked on this international business. We were 14 IMPs ahead as the second set started. The other Polish pair were quite young, even younger than Nicola and me.

I missed a chance on this deal, where I was sitting West:

North–South game
Dealer West

	North	
	♠ A Q 7 6 3 ♡ A Q ♢ 10 4 2 ♣ Q 10 5	
West ♠ 4 ♡ J 9 6 5 ♢ K Q 9 7 5 3 ♣ 9 2	N W E S	**East** ♠ K J 10 9 5 ♡ K 8 4 ♢ 8 6 ♣ 8 7 4
	♠ 8 2 ♡ 10 7 3 2 ♢ A J ♣ A K J 6 3	
	South	

West	*North*	*East*	*South*
Debbie	Jadwiga Dolowa	Nicola	Urszula Krogulska
Pass	1♠	Pass	2♣
2♢	3♣	Pass	3NT
All Pass			

A diamond lead would have given them nine easy tricks. I started well enough by leading a heart, dummy's queen losing to the king. Nicola switched to ♢8 and I won declarer's jack with the queen. I didn't like to risk a diamond back in case declarer was trying to trick me from an initial holding of ♢AJ6. I exited with a low heart to the bare ace in dummy and declarer proceeded to cash five rounds of clubs. These cards were still to be played:

	Jadwiga ♠ A Q 7 ♡ – ♢ 10 4 ♣ –	
Debbie ♠ 4 ♡ J 9 ♢ K 9 ♣ –	N W E S	*Nicola* ♠ K J 10 ♡ 4 ♢ 6 ♣ –
	♠ 8 2 ♡ 10 7 ♢ A ♣ – *Urszula*	

The South player, a pretty girl who couldn't have been more than 22 or so, paused to consider what to do next. No doubt she could place me with a 4–6 shape in the red suits; I had followed to two clubs so I was marked with a singleton spade. Eventually she cashed the ace of diamonds, played a spade to the ace, and exited with a diamond. With a sinking feeling I won with the bare king. I now had to concede a ninth trick to declarer's ♡10.

I could have beaten the contract by returning a diamond earlier in the play. Worse than that, I realised now that there had been no point at all in keeping that spade. Had I come down to ♡J9 and three diamonds, I could have discarded ♡9 when declarer crossed to the spade ace.

Quite an amazing hand occurred later in this set.

Game all
Dealer West

	North	
	♠ A K 7 4 ♡ A 8 4 ◇ K 8 7 4 3 ♣ 4	
West ♠ J 10 ♡ J 10 7 6 5 2 ◇ Q ♣ Q 6 5 3	N / W E / S	**East** ♠ Q 8 5 2 ♡ – ◇ A 10 9 6 5 ♣ 9 8 7 2
	♠ 9 6 3 ♡ K Q 9 3 ◇ J 2 ♣ A K J 10	

West	*North*	*East*	*South*
Debbie	Jadwiga Dolowa	Nicola	Urszula Krogulska
Pass	1◇	Pass	1♡
Pass	1♠	Pass	3NT
All Pass			

I resisted the temptation to open a multi on my hand and the opponents ended in 3NT. South obviously had the clubs fairly well held, so I tried my luck with the jack of spades. Krogulska, whose black hair was tied back in a pony tail, won with the ace and finessed the jack of clubs. I took the queen and played a second spade to dummy's king.

Krogulska now had eight top tricks, with an easy ninth should either of the majors break 3–3. 'Small spade,' she said, in a rather heavy accent.

Nicola won with the queen and proceeded to cash the ♠8. She then exited with a club and declarer cashed the remainder of that suit. Krogulska probably thought it was all over when she saw my two heart discards, but when she cashed the king of hearts Nicola showed out; I still had the suit guarded. This was the ending:

Jadwiga
♠ –
♡ A 8
◇ K 8
♣ –

Debbie
♠ –
♡ J 10 7
◇ Q
♣ –

N / W E / S

Nicola
♠ –
♡ –
◇ A 10 9 5
♣ –

♠ –
♡ Q 9 3
◇ J
♣ –
Urszula

A diamond towards the king would work now if I held the ace. Unfortunately for us, Krogulska had spotted a line that would succeed whether I held the ace or queen of diamonds. She led ♡3 from hand and I had to insert the jack to prevent her finessing the 8. 'Ace,' said Krogulska. 'And diamond eight.'

It was all over for us. Nicola could see that if she won with the ace she would have to concede a trick to dummy's king of diamonds. She played low instead but then I had to win with the queen and lead back into declarer's ♡Q9. I don't know what name you would give to that ending but the effect was disastrous, 600 in the minus column.

Krogulska turned towards me, her eyes filled with delight. 'Good hand, yes?' she said.

I smiled back. 'Yes,' I replied. 'Incredible.'

We lost several IMPs on that set but recovered strongly in the next two sets. Nicola did well on this one:

Love all
Dealer South

	North	
	♠ 5 2 ♡ K J 8 ♢ K J 9 5 4 3 ♣ 6 2	
♠ K Q 10 3 ♡ A Q 10 6 ♢ Q 7 6 ♣ A 10	N / W E / S	♠ 9 8 7 4 ♡ 9 4 2 ♢ 2 ♣ K 9 5 4 3
	♠ A J 6 ♡ 7 5 3 ♢ A 10 8 ♣ Q J 8 7	

West	*North*	*East*	*South*
Irene Pukowska	Debbie	Maria Frycz	Nicola
–	–	–	1♣
Dble	1♢	Pass	1NT
Pass	2♢	2♠	Pass
Pass	3♢	Pass	3NT
Dble	All Pass		

When I went to three diamonds I was only competing for the part score, of course. Nicola took this a little too seriously and we arrived in 3NT with just 20 points between the two hands.

Pukowska doubled and led the king of spades; East played the 4 and South the 6. The way Nicola and I signal, the 4 would have been a discouraging card and West would have had to switch (not that there was an obvious switch). Our luck was in when, for some reason, Pukowska continued with the spade queen at trick 2. Nicola won with the ace and paused for thought. West doubtless held the ace of hearts, and could be finessed for the diamond queen. The only problem was how to cash the second spade trick without establishing five winners for the defence. Deciding to retain the diamond ace as an entry to her hand, Nicola led ♢10 at trick 3.

Had West failed to cover, Nicola would have run the 10 successfully and established her ninth trick with a heart to the king; the ace of diamonds would be the entry to cash the second spade winner. Perhaps sensing this, Pukowska covered ♢10 with the queen, won by dummy's king.

There was now no safe way to score two spade tricks and a heart. Nicola concluded that she would need to make two heart tricks. She returned to the diamond ace, and led a heart to the jack. When this card held, it was all over. She came back to her hand with ♢8 and played a heart to the king. Moments later, we were writing a precious +550 on our scorecards.

'Ah, you had the club king, Maria,' exclaimed Pukowska. 'I have to underlead club ace at trick 2. Only way to beat it.'

A lengthy discussion in Polish followed, doubtless on their signalling in the spade suit. They were leading the king from both AK and KQ. Perhaps West thought partner might discourage from J874, in case the lead was from an AK holding.

Not that we cared. Nicola and I were performing really well; it seemed to inspire us, playing with really good players. Pat and Judy must have been quite surprised not to find any minus 800s on our card.

'We're 23 IMPs up,' declared Pat Draper happily. 'Quite a useful lead with only 8 boards to go.'

21 Up and Away

There were a good dozen spectators around each of the tables as the last set of the match began. Irene Pukowska, the Polish captain, found an annoying defence against me on this board:

Game all
Dealer South

	North	
	♠ 8 4 ♡ A Q 4 ◇ J 9 4 3 ♣ A K 7 5	
West ♠ 10 7 5 3 2 ♡ 9 7 6 ◇ A 5 ♣ J 9 8	N / W E / S	**East** ♠ K Q J ♡ 10 8 5 2 ◇ 8 6 ♣ Q 10 6 4
	♠ A 9 6 ♡ K J 3 ◇ K Q 10 7 2 ♣ 3 2	
	South	

West	*North*	*East*	*South*
Maria Frycz	Nicola	Irene Pukowska	Debbie
–	–	–	1NT
Pass	3NT	All Pass	

Five diamonds would have been a better contract, as you can see. Anyway, we reached 3NT and West led ♠2. East played the queen on the first trick, which I allowed to hold. Next came the king of spades.

I really don't see how I could have read the situation. I ducked again, of course, hoping to exhaust East's spades and then find her with the ace of diamonds. I felt a bit sick when East now produced the jack of spades. I won and played on diamonds but West leapt in with the ace and cashed two more spades, putting the contract one down.

'It was a clever defence,' I explained to Nicola. 'If she plays the jack of spades on the first trick, then the king, it would be obvious for me to block the suit by winning the second round.'

Irene Pukowska gave me a sympathetic smile. 'It is a normal deception with king-queen-jack,' she said. 'Your East does the same, I am sure.'

They produced another sharp defence a board or two later.

North–South game
Dealer West

	North	
	♠ 10 9 3 ♡ A 6 ◇ Q J 8 ♣ A K 10 9 3	
West ♠ A J ♡ 10 8 3 ◇ A K 9 7 6 5 4 ♣ 8	N / W E / S	**East** ♠ 7 4 ♡ J 9 7 5 4 ◇ 2 ♣ J 7 5 4 2
	♠ K Q 8 6 5 2 ♡ K Q 2 ◇ 10 3 ♣ Q 6	

West	*North*	*East*	*South*
Maria Frycz	Nicola	Irene Pukowska	Debbie
1◇	2♣	Pass	2♠
3◇	3♠	Pass	4♠
All Pass			

We reached four spades and Frycz led the ace of diamonds, drawing the 2 from her partner. If East had as little as a singleton 8 of trumps, two more rounds of diamonds would now beat the contract. East would ruff the third round with the 8, forcing a high honour from declarer, and West's AJ of trumps would then be worth two tricks.

Frycz could see a much better chance – at trick 2 she switched to her singleton club. I won with the queen and led the king of trumps. Frycz took the ace and underled her king of diamonds, forcing East to ruff. Back came a club, ruffed by West and that was one down.

I looked resignedly at the blonde-cropped West player. 'You did well,' I said.

Frycz gave a modest shrug. 'No, it was easy to see,' she replied.

The next two or three hands produced nothing good for us and I had a nasty feeling that our lead in the match had been whittled away. Then, from out of the blue, this monster hand arrived:

Game all
Dealer South

	North	
	♠ J 9 8 2 ♡ 10 8 7 5 2 ◇ K ♣ J 10 7	
West ♠ – ♡ K Q J 9 6 ◇ 10 8 6 5 2 ♣ K 8 2	N / W E / S	**East** ♠ 7 6 4 ♡ A 4 3 ◇ 9 7 ♣ Q 9 6 4 3
	♠ A K Q 10 5 3 ♡ – ◇ A Q J 4 3 ♣ A 5	

West	*North*	*East*	*South*
Maria Frycz	Nicola	Irene Pukowska	Debbie
–	–	–	2♣
2♡	Pass	Pass	2♠
Pass	3♠	Pass	4♣
Pass	4◇	Pass	4NT
Pass	5♣	Pass	5NT
Pass	6◇	Pass	7♠
All Pass			

Nicola and I cue-bid all controls alike, so her 4◇ might have been on a singleton or void. I needed her to hold the king of diamonds, rather than a shortage, to bid the grand, and this could be determined with Roman Key-Card Blackwood. My follow-up of 5NT asked her to cue-bid any king she held and the 6◇ response showed the card I was looking for. My heart pounding, I reached into the bidding box for the 7♠ card. Yes, this was life in the fast lane!

Maria Frycz led the king of hearts and Nicola laid out her dummy. I recalled a piece of advice that Jeremy Flint had given in his classic book, *Tiger Bridge*. When a really big hand comes along you should award it an appropriate amount of effort. What had he called it? Operation Big Deal – that was it.

If trumps were 2–1 all would be well; I could discard dummy's club losers on my diamonds and ruff a club and a diamond in dummy. If trumps were 3–0 and the diamonds 4–3, I'd be OK again – I would need only one ruff in the dummy. So, what could be done if both the trumps and the diamonds broke badly?

Eventually I saw it. I should play for a dummy reversal. If I could ruff four of dummy's hearts in the South hand, I would be able to draw trumps in the dummy. The three remaining losers in dummy could be discarded on the diamond suit.

I'd spent so long thinking about the hand that Nicola was looking quite anxious. I gave her a reassuring smile. 'Small, please,' I said.

I ruffed the heart lead with the ace and crossed to dummy with a trump to the jack, West showing out. After another heart ruffed high, I crossed to the 9 of trumps. A third high heart ruff was followed by a diamond to the king and a fourth heart ruff with my last trump. The lead was in the South hand and these cards remained:

Nicola
♠ 8 2
♡ 10
♢ –
♣ J 10 7

Maria		*Irene*
♠ –	N	♠ 7
♡ Q	W E	♡ –
♢ 10 8 6 5	S	♢ 7
♣ K		♣ Q 9 6 4

♠ –
♡ –
♢ A Q J 4
♣ A 5
Debbie

I ruffed ♢4 to reach dummy and drew East's last trump, discarding a club from my hand. It was a moment to savour as I spread my last four cards on the table – my hand was high.

Sensing that the match was lost, Irene Pukowska swept up her cards and returned them to the wallet. 'Unfortunate lead, partner,' she said. 'Lead anything else, she cannot ruff so many hearts.'

Draper and Sharman looked up anxiously as we rejoined them. 'What happened on the big hand?' asked Judy Sharman. 'You bid the unlucky grand?'

'Yes,' said Nicola, dropping into one of the spare chairs.

'It could be close, then,' said Pat Draper. 'We interfered too much and they stopped in six.'

'Debbie made the grand,' said Nicola.

'You made it?' exclaimed Judy Sharman. 'That's brilliant, Debbie! We must have done enough in that case.'

She was right. We had won the match by 13 IMPs. 'You girls played very well,' declared Pat Draper, as she gave me a congratulatory embrace. 'Very well, indeed.'

We spent a great evening with the Polish team, recounting old stories and sharing various bottles of vodka they had brought with them. I felt absolutely marvellous as I staggered back to my room. It had been the best day of my life by a mile.

Men? Who needs them?